A

Policing
the Internet

Policing the Internet

Alan Marzilli

SERIES CONSULTING EDITOR
Alan Marzilli, M.A., J.D.

CHELSEA HOUSE
PUBLISHERS

A Haights Cross Communications Company

Philadelphia

CHELSEA HOUSE PUBLISHERS

VP, New Product Development Sally Cheney
Director of Production Kim Shinners
Creative Manager Takeshi Takahashi
Manufacturing Manager Diann Grasse

Staff for POLICING THE INTERNET

Executive Editor Lee Marcott
Editor Kate Sullivan
Photo Editor Sarah Bloom
Production Editor Noelle Nardone
Series and Cover Designer Keith Trego
Layout 21st Century Publishing and Communications, Inc.

A Haights Cross Communications ◢ Company

http://www.chelseahouse.com

First Printing

1 3 5 7 9 8 6 4 2

Library of Congress Cataloging-in-Publication Data

Marzilli, Alan.
    Policing the Internet / Alan Marzilli.
        p. cm.—(Point-counterpoint)
    Includes bibliographical references and index.
    ISBN 0-7910-8088-9
    1. Computer crimes—United States—Prevention. 2. Internet—Law and legislation—
United States. 3. Internet—Government policy—United States. I. Title.
II. Point-counterpoint (Philadelphia, Pa.)
    HV6773.2.M37 2004
    343.7309'944—dc22

                                                            2004011554

All links and web addresses were checked and verified to be correct at the time of
publication. Because of the dynamic nature of the web, some addresses and links
may have changed since publication and may no longer be valid.

CONTENTS

Foreword

Alan Marzilli, M.A., J.D.
Durham, North Carolina

The debates presented in POINT/COUNTERPOINT are among the most interesting and controversial in contemporary American society, but studying them is more than an academic activity. They affect every citizen; they are the issues that today's leaders debate and tomorrow's will decide. The reader may one day play a central role in resolving them.

Why study both sides of the debate? It's possible that the reader will not yet have formed any opinion at all on the subject of this volume—but this is unlikely. It is more likely that the reader will already hold an opinion, probably a strong one, and very probably one formed without full exposure to the arguments of the other side. It is rare to hear an argument presented in a balanced way, and it is easy to form an opinion on too little information; these books will help to fill in the informational gaps that can never be avoided. More important, though, is the practical function of the series: Skillful argumentation requires a thorough knowledge of *both* sides—though there are seldom only two, and only by knowing what an opponent is likely to assert can one form an articulate response.

Perhaps more important is that listening to the other side sometimes helps one to see an opponent's arguments in a more human way. For example, Sister Helen Prejean, one of the nation's most visible opponents of capital punishment, has been deeply affected by her interactions with the families of murder victims. Seeing the families' grief and pain, she understands much better why people support the death penalty, and she is able to carry out her advocacy with a greater sensitivity to the needs and beliefs of those who do not agree with her. Her relativism, in turn, lends credibility to her work. Dismissing the other side of the argument as totally without merit can be too easy—it is far more useful to understand the nature of the controversy and the reasons *why* the issue defies resolution.

The most controversial issues of all are often those that center on a constitutional right. The Bill of Rights—the first ten amendments to the U.S. Constitution—spells out some of the most fundamental rights that distinguish the governmental system of the United States from those that allow fewer (or other) freedoms. But the sparsely worded document is open to interpretation, and clauses of only a few words are often at the heart of national debates. The Bill of Rights was meant to protect individual liberties; but the needs of some individuals clash with those of society as a whole, and when this happens someone has to decide where to draw the line. Thus the Constitution becomes a battleground between the rights of individuals to do as they please and the responsibility of the government to protect its citizens. The First Amendment's guarantee of "freedom of speech," for example, leads to a number of difficult questions. Some forms of expression, such as burning an American flag, lead to public outrage—but nevertheless are said to be protected by the First Amendment. Other types of expression that most people find objectionable, such as sexually explicit material involving children, are not protected because they are considered harmful. The question is not only where to draw the line, but how to do this without infringing on the personal liberties on which the United States was built.

The Bill of Rights raises many other questions about individual rights and the societal "good." Is a prayer before a high school football game an "establishment of religion" prohibited by the First Amendment? Does the Second Amendment's promise of "the right to bear arms" include concealed handguns? Is stopping and frisking someone standing on a corner known to be frequented by drug dealers a form of "unreasonable search and seizure" in violation of the Fourth Amendment? Although the nine-member U.S. Supreme Court has the ultimate authority in interpreting the Constitution, its answers do not always satisfy the public. When a group of nine people—sometimes by a five-to-four vote—makes a decision that affects the lives of hundreds of millions, public outcry can be expected. And the composition of the Court does change over time, so even a landmark decision is not guaranteed to stand forever. The limits of constitutional protection are always in flux.

These issues make headlines, divide courts, and decide elections. They are the questions most worthy of national debate, and this series aims to cover them as thoroughly as possible. Each volume sets out some of the key arguments surrounding a particular issue, even some views that most people consider extreme or radical—but presents a balanced perspective on the issue. Excerpts from the relevant laws and judicial opinions and references to central concepts, source material, and advocacy groups help the reader to explore the issues even further and to read "the letter of the law" just as the legislatures and the courts have established it.

It may seem that some debates—such as those over capital punishment and abortion, debates with a strong moral component—will never be resolved. But American history offers numerous examples of controversies that once seemed insurmountable but now are effectively settled, even if only on the surface. Abolitionists met with widespread resistance to their efforts to end slavery, and the controversy over that issue threatened to cleave the nation in two; but today public debate over the merits of slavery would be unthinkable, though racial inequalities still plague the nation. Similarly unthinkable at one time was suffrage for women and minorities, but this is now a matter of course. Distributing information about contraception once was a crime. Societies change, and attitudes change, and new questions of social justice are raised constantly while the old ones fade into irrelevancy.

Whatever the root of the controversy, the books in POINT/ COUNTERPOINT seek to explain to the reader the origins of the debate, the current state of the law, and the arguments on both sides. The goal of the series is to inform the reader about the issues facing not only American politicians, but all of the nation's citizens, and to encourage the reader to become more actively involved in resolving these debates, as a voter, a concerned citizen, a journalist, an activist, or an elected official. Democracy is based on education, and every voice counts—so every opinion must be an informed one.

New technologies can present problems for judges and lawmakers, who frequently attempt to regulate new technologies that they do not fully understand. The Internet has been especially problematic for regulators because its low cost and versatility helped its use to boom at an unprecedented pace. By its very nature, the Internet is difficult to regulate because nobody owns it, and therefore anybody can access it from anywhere in the world and do so anonymously. Even when someone does something others consider objectionable—such as posting pornography, sharing copyrighted music, or sending annoying junk e-mails—it is often difficult to catch the culprit. Many civil libertarians think that the Internet should not be regulated at all, and that free speech and free trade should be the order of the day. However, many conservatives see the Internet as a moral threat, and music companies view sharing music as piracy. Almost everyone would like to receive fewer junk e-mail messages. This volume examines government efforts to police the Internet and the ongoing debate between supporters of free speech and those who think that the Internet has gone too far.

When Technology Moves Faster Than the Law

I n 1995, a graduate of the University of Michigan was engaged in a relatively new pastime—surfing the Internet—when he discovered some very troubling material and reported it to the university. College student Jake Baker was using his University of Michigan Internet account to post graphic stories about rape, torture, and murder to an Internet newsgroup called "alt.sex.stories." One of the stories named a classmate as the object of a particularly brutal attack, during which he and a friend rape her; assault her with a hairbrush, curling iron, and knife; and set fire to her apartment as they leave her to die. Baker later turned over to the police e-mail messages in which he and an unidentified Canadian discussed a desire to commit similar acts in the near future upon unnamed victims, including kidnapping a female college student and a teenage girl.

Baker's violent messages came to the attention of the general public at a time when people knew very little about the Internet, a vast system of computers linked together—in those days—primarily by telephone lines. The network had many applications, including one-on-one communication through e-mail, publishing written materials to open newsgroups, and the World Wide Web, which offered primarily text and pictures. Quickly, individual users, universities, and profit-seeking companies sought new applications for the Internet, transforming it into the broad array of multimedia, shopping, auctions, and news that attracted tens of millions of new users. At the time, Baker's case seemed to pose new questions to a justice system and a public that did not yet fully understand how the Internet worked or what impact it would have on society. The case raised questions about how the legal system should police the Internet, and even today new questions arise almost as fast as old questions are answered.

- **How would you react if someone wrote a story about murdering you? Should that person be put in prison?**

The Unsuccessful Prosecution of Jake Baker

Because of Baker's e-mails and newsgroup stories, the university suspended him, and a Federal Bureau of Investigation (FBI) inquiry led prosecutors to file federal charges against him. Baker's classmate did not learn of the newsgroup story about her until the investigation started and she began hearing from law enforcement officials and journalists. The classmate, who had never spoken with Baker, was obviously very disturbed by the revelations, and the incident sparked outrage on the campus and across the nation.

Baker spent time behind bars awaiting trial but was released after the charges against him were dismissed by a federal judge in Detroit. Judge Avern Cohn noted that the First Amendment to the U.S. Constitution, which protects freedom of speech, prohibits prosecuting violent messages unless they are direct threats. He wrote:

> The government's enthusiastic beginning petered out to a salvage effort once it recognized that the communication which so much alarmed the University of Michigan officials was only a rather savage and tasteless piece of fiction. Why the government became involved in the matter is not really explained in the record. . . . Whatever Baker's faults, and he is to be faulted, he did not violate [federal law]. The case would have been better handled [by the university] as a disciplinary matter.[1]

Disappointed with Judge Cohn's ruling, prosecutors appealed the decision, and the classmate described in the story filed an amicus ("friend of the court") brief authored by University of Michigan law professor and noted feminist Catherine MacKinnon. Professor MacKinnon argued that holding Baker accountable for his hateful words did not threaten free speech, writing that First Amendment limits on laws prohibiting threats were designed to protect "dissenting political advocacy, which is often expressed as virulent hostility to government officials and agencies."[2] In her opinion, the First Amendment protects writing about overthrowing the government but not writing about raping, torturing, and murdering a classmate, whose name is then exposed to pornography users throughout the world.

MacKinnon argued that although the prosecution did not threaten Baker's constitutional rights, dismissing the charges threatened the rights of women. Noting that courts had upheld prosecutions for publishing threats of violence against the president of the United States, MacKinnon argued that dismissing charges against Baker resulted in unequal treatment of women. She wrote:

> [The prosecutors] applied existing legal standards that fit the facts as if women count as citizens, without stereotyping

them as sex objects freely available for threat of violation—
threats that the perpetrators also sexually enjoyed. The United
States proceeded as if a threat of injury to a woman, albeit
sexual, is every bit as threatening as a threat of injury to a
man, even if that man is the President of the United States.
This Court should not permit effective nullification for
women only of the law of threat.[3]

• Can speech violate the rights of all women? Of all minorities?

Not surprisingly, the American Civil Liberties Union
(ACLU) came to Baker's defense with its own brief. The ACLU
staunchly defends the First Amendment right to free speech,
even when the speech in question is offensive to many, such as
during Ku Klux Klan rallies or Baker's newsgroup stories and
e-mail messages. The ACLU argued that the prosecution of
Baker violated his First Amendment rights, claiming:

> This is a case of "pure speech." No immediate harm results
> from the expression of a desire to commit a crime. The only
> warrant for proscribing such expression is the possibility that
> it will produce harm, should the speaker act on his desire, in
> the future. An assertion of intent or desire unattended by any
> immediate harm is an utterance falling within the broad range
> of communications to which the First Amendment applies.[4]

Although the civil liberties group acknowledged that the
government has the power to prosecute actual threats, it argued
that threats must be narrowly defined in order to protect the
right of citizens to express their feelings, no matter how offensive
they might be to others. Citing earlier Supreme Court decisions,
the ACLU wrote:

> In a case where a speaker urges others to violate the law,
> the constitutional guarantee of free speech will not permit

proscription of such advocacy except where it "is directed to inciting or producing imminent lawless action and is likely to induce or produce such action". . . . The danger must be clear. It must be present. It must be immediately likely to be realized. It must be imminent.[5]

In the ACLU's opinion, Baker's writings, though offensive, did not constitute a "clear and present danger" to any specific person. The brief argued: "Whatever danger the messages in the present case even arguably embody does not approximate what is required to justify criminal prosecution." Ultimately, a federal appeals court agreed with Baker and the ACLU, upholding Judge Cohn's decision to dismiss the charges.

A War for Control Over the Internet

Although the federal government lost its battle against Jake Baker, it continued to mount a war against the rising tide of material on the Internet that many people found objectionable. Baker's writings might have been an extreme example, but many parents began discovering to their disgust that their children were using the family computer not for homework, or even innocent pleasures like video games, but to access the growing store of pornography available online. Parents, religious groups, and conservative politicians began to express concern that the vast network of linked computers would fall into a state of anarchy unless lawmakers acted swiftly and convincingly.

In 1996, after reading dozens of angry complaints from parents on the House and Senate floors, Congress passed the Communications Decency Act (CDA). In addition to material being shared by e-mail and on newsgroups—like Jake Baker's writings—thousands of new websites were offering pornography, including a staggering number of sites offering illegal child pornography. The CDA was a sweeping law, effectively banishing any "indecent" material from the Internet—including the World Wide Web, newsgroups, and e-mail—by imposing criminal

FROM THE BENCH

The Supreme Court Confronts the Internet for the First Time

When the Supreme Court listened to arguments in Reno v. ACLU *in 1997, the law relating to the Internet was unsettled, and many legal experts were unsure how the Court would decide to regulate free speech on the Internet. In a decision striking the federal Communications Decency Act, the justices expressed awe for the Internet's communicative potential:*

Anyone with access to the Internet may take advantage of a wide variety of communication and information retrieval methods. These methods are constantly evolving and difficult to categorize precisely. But, as presently constituted, those most relevant to this case are electronic mail ("e-mail"), automatic mailing list services ("mail exploders," sometimes referred to as "listservs"), "newsgroups," "chat rooms," and the "World Wide Web." All of these methods can be used to transmit text; most can transmit sound, pictures, and moving video images. Taken together, these tools constitute a unique medium—known to its users as "cyberspace"—located in no particular geographical location but available to anyone, anywhere in the world, with access to the Internet. . . .

The District Court found that at any given time "tens of thousands of users are engaging in conversations on a huge range of subjects." It is "no exaggeration to conclude that the content on the Internet is as diverse as human thought." From the publishers' point of view, it constitutes a vast platform from which to address and hear from a worldwide audience of millions of readers, viewers, researchers, and buyers. Any person or organization with a computer connected to the Internet can "publish" information. Publishers include government agencies, educational institutions, commercial entities, advocacy groups, and individuals.

Publishers may either make their material available to the entire pool of Internet users or confine access to a selected group, such as those willing to pay for the privilege. "No single organization controls any membership in the Web, nor is there any centralized point from which individual websites or services can be blocked from the Web."

Source: *Reno v. ACLU*, 521 U.S. 884 (1997)

penalties for letting such materials reach minors. Material that would be considered legal in movie theaters, magazines, letters, phone calls, and even cable TV was criminalized by the CDA. Civil libertarian groups such as the ACLU challenged the law immediately, and the Supreme Court ruled unanimously that the law violated the First Amendment. Writing for seven of the nine justices, John Paul Stevens noted the chilling effect that the CDA had on the growing "marketplace of ideas" available online:

> The Government apparently assumes that the unregulated availability of "indecent" and "patently offensive" material on the Internet is driving countless citizens away from the medium because of the risk of exposing themselves or their children to harmful material. We find this argument singularly unpersuasive. The dramatic expansion of this new marketplace of ideas contradicts the factual basis of this contention. The record demonstrates that the growth of the Internet has been and continues to be phenomenal. As a matter of constitutional tradition, in the absence of evidence to the contrary, we presume that governmental regulation of the content of speech is more likely to interfere with the free exchange of ideas than to encourage it. The interest in encouraging freedom of expression in a democratic society outweighs any theoretical but unproven benefit of censorship.[7]

The government's complete and convincing defeat in the CDA case nevertheless seemed to strengthen some lawmakers' resolve to protect children from offensive materials on the Internet.

• Does pornography contribute to a "marketplace of ideas"?

At the center of any First Amendment free speech debate is the medium in which the speech is delivered or, in legal jargon, the type of "forum." Television and radio, because they rely on the use of public airwaves, are held to a much higher standard than newspapers, magazines, and cable television. Speech in public schools is held to even stricter standards. In general, public ownership of a forum—whether it is the airwaves, the public schools, or the courthouse steps—justifies tighter restrictions. Courts and lawmakers have struggled to put boundaries on Internet speech because the major unanswered question is, "Who owns the Internet?"

Initially, the Internet grew out of a computer network developed by the Department of Defense; however, many additional privately owned computers joined the network, making it impossible to argue that the federal government owned the Internet. At first, most connections were made by telephone line, perhaps making possible an argument that phone companies had an ownership interest in the Internet. New technologies like cable and fiber optic lines boosted the speed of the Internet.

Helping to connect individual users to the Internet are Internet service providers (ISPs). Some ISPs were private companies operating for a profit—early examples included Prodigy, CompuServe, and America Online, with Earthlink and Microsoft's MSN later capturing large chunks of the market. Many universities operate as their own ISPs, providing both the connection lines and the computer technology. Most ISPs also run servers, which are large computers storing the computer data of websites as well as storing e-mails and newsgroup messages. Some have argued that ISPs own a stake in the Internet because they use their money to store the Internet's data on servers and to transmit the data on various types of data lines. As more data is transmitted, ISPs must invest in more lines, thereby increasing their "bandwidth," or capacity to transmit data.

With the World Wide Web, most data was stored on servers owned by ISPs, universities, or corporations—typically on large, fast computers that were set aside for use only as servers. In recent years, however, a new technology called "peer-to-peer," or P2P for short, has emerged. When people log on to these networks, their home computers act as smaller servers. At first, the most popular of these P2P networks was the Napster network, which allowed users to share music files. This practice raised another concern among lawmakers: Most of the songs traded on Napster were traded without the permission of the songwriters or performers, and therefore, the creators of the music were denied the opportunity to profit from the downloading of their music.

The boom in popularity of Napster and of the other P2P networks that popped up after courts shut down Napster (later reborn as a legitimate paid service) highlighted a major problem. The speed of modern Internet connections enabled easy copying of information that was protected by federal and international copyright laws, which give creators of art and literature the right to control how their materials are distributed and to make money from their sale. Music, movies, video games, word-processing programs, books, and magazines, however, could be copied with relative ease and shared on the Internet, frustrating the efforts of filmmakers, songwriters, musicians, and authors to profit from their own hard work. Congress responded by passing the Digital Millennium Copyright Act, which offers legal remedies to copyright owners. Stopping the copying is another matter entirely. Because of the speed, anonymity, and widespread availability of the Internet, millions of songs, movies, and television shows are copied daily, leaving many wondering if anything really can be done. Some even argue that copying and distributing copyrighted material should be allowed under law—and even encouraged.

E-mail presents a different problem. Although it is extremely versatile, quick, and cheap, many people think that the promise of e-mail to support a communications revolution is threatened by the explosion of junk e-mail or "spam." Although Internet users almost universally despise spam, its regulation raises questions of both ownership and free speech. Spammers say that it is within their First Amendment right to send e-mails to whomever they choose. Many ISPs have asserted that spammers are trampling upon their property. ISPs spend millions of dollars on increasing bandwidth and purchasing servers to store e-mail. As more spam is sent to the ISPs' subscribers, they must bear the costs of server capacity and bandwidth—costs that they ultimately pass on to their subscribers.

Never before has a phenomenon like the Internet so overwhelmed the nation's courts and legislatures. With rapid advances in technology, judges and legislators simply cannot keep pace with the changes. The questions of Internet regulation raise many issues of free speech and property rights. Some are easier to resolve, such as when people use the Internet to commit fraud or other traditional crimes. Legislators have taken a firm stance on hacking or using computers to disrupt or steal others' information, but catching hackers remains difficult. On issues such as regulating pornography, song swapping, and spam, legislators and courts have struggled to come up with regulations that are both effective and constitutional.

———●———————●———————●———

Summary

Although the Internet poses many new technological issues, its use also touches upon established principles of law, including free speech, copyright, and property rights. Courts have struggled to apply these older legal principles to the newer technology, and strategies for policing the Internet remain intensely controversial.

Censoring the Internet Threatens Freedom of Speech

During the latter half of the 1990s, the Internet's popularity exploded. Unlike previous technological revolutions, which relied on a few wealthy industrialists to fund developments, anybody with a computer and a modem had access to the Internet, and those with the knowledge and interest could shape the Internet into just about anything they wanted it to be. Not surprisingly, the Internet attracted many young people, and by the time their parents found out what was going on, they were not too happy with the types of material children could access online.

The widespread availability of pornography on the Internet caused a great deal of alarm among parents, religious leaders, conservatives, and feminists. Sensing a chance to win points with their constituencies, many politicians, particularly conservative politicians, jumped on the Internet-bashing bandwagon. As part of a major reform of communications law, the U.S. Congress passed the Communications Decency Act (CDA) of 1996, which made it a federal crime to transmit "obscene or indecent" material to anyone under 18 years of age.

Many civil libertarians accused Congress of passing a blatantly unconstitutional law. The First Amendment to the U.S. Constitution provides that "Congress shall make no law . . . abridging the freedom of speech." Critics accused members of Congress of passing a law that was in clear violation of the First Amendment, knowing that courts would strike down the law. Passing the law, however, allowed the members of Congress to tell their constituents that they were trying to do something about Internet indecency but that "those darn courts" would not let them.

Although the Supreme Court had held that "obscene" materials did not enjoy the protection of the First Amendment, obscenity describes a very limited category of materials, and the CDA sought to banish a much larger category of material from the Internet, prohibiting "indecent" material as well. While in everyday terms, the difference between "obscene" and "indecent" might seem slight, the two are quite different in legal terms. For something to be obscene, it must be completely without artistic or literary value. In general, material that is obscene may not legally be distributed anywhere. On the other hand, the term "indecent" has generally referred to standards for broadcast television and radio. Because television stations are licensed to use public airwaves, courts have upheld strict regulations on television content, but cable movie channels have for years shown "indecent" material. In effect, the CDA would have held the Internet to stricter standards than cable television.

Not surprisingly, in *Reno* v. *ACLU* the Supreme Court voted overwhelmingly to declare the CDA unconstitutional, with seven justices joining John Paul Stevens's opinion and all nine justices agreeing that the law's censorship of the World Wide

Web was unconstitutional. Noting that the CDA hampered free speech in cyberspace, Justice Stevens wrote:

> This dynamic, multifaceted category of communication includes not only traditional print and news services, but also audio, video, and still images, as well as interactive, real time dialogue. Through the use of chat rooms, any person with a phone line can become a town crier with a voice that resonates farther than it could from any soapbox. Through the use of Web pages, mail exploders, and newsgroups, the same individual can become a pamphleteer. . . . Could a speaker confidently assume that a serious discussion about birth control practices, homosexuality, . . . First Amendment issues . . . or the consequences of prison rape would not violate the CDA? . . . In order to deny minors access to potentially harmful speech, the CDA effectively suppresses a large amount of speech that adults have a constitutional right to receive and to address to one another.[8]

The *Reno* v. *ACLU* ruling, however, did not end the debate on regulating the content of material on the Internet as conservative politicians, concerned parents, religious groups, and others united to pass further laws attempting to regulate free expression on the Internet. Although courts have generally frowned upon efforts to restrict content on the Internet, federal prosecutors have renewed their commitment to combat online pornography. Some worry that closed-minded communities will try to impose their conservative values on the global communications network of the Internet. Additionally, a ruling by the Supreme Court allows the federal government to require—as a "string" attached to federal funding—public libraries to install "filtering" software.[9] Civil libertarians have redoubled their efforts to fight all types of Internet censorship, arguing that adult pornography is a harmless activity and that libraries should refuse federal funding rather than censoring patrons' Internet access.

Efforts to combat adult pornography unreasonably target a victimless activity.

In the first few years after the Communications Decency Act was declared unconstitutional, most of the law enforcement efforts against Internet pornography were directed against child pornography. The illegality of child pornography—in contrast to pornography featuring adult models—is well established. While the Supreme Court has noted a constitutional right to view adult pornography in the privacy of the home, a similar right does not exist for child pornography because the creation of child pornography involves criminal exploitation of children. Therefore, the market for child pornography encourages illegal activity. Additionally, prosecutors have generated good publicity by combating child pornography because an overwhelming majority of people are repulsed by it, and few people are willing to publicly support a right to view child pornography. A group of adult websites has even formed a coalition, Adult Sites Against Child Pornography (ASACP) to help fight the proliferation of child pornography on the Internet.

In recent years, some states have stepped up efforts to combat pornography featuring adult models, and under the leadership of conservative Attorney General John Ashcroft, the U.S. Department of Justice has also taken a renewed interest in adult pornography. Such efforts have angered many people who believe that adults should have the right to view pornography featuring adult models. Unlike child pornography, which exploits unwilling victims, the vast majority of adult pornography features people who knowingly and willingly participated in making the pornography in exchange for money. Supporters say that adult pornography prosecutions target a "victimless crime" and that obscenity laws should be abolished, with only child pornography remaining illegal.

- **Is pornography a victimless activity?**

Although conservatives and some feminists say that all pornography leads to harm, such as disrespect and violence against women, many defenders of free expression—including pornography—maintain that there is no sound evidence that pornography is harmful. Even if it were harmful, ACLU president Nadine Strossen believes, people should not have to prove that their speech is harmless. She writes, "[We] would have no free speech . . . were such a burden of proof actually to be imposed on those seeking to enjoy their liberties."[10] She notes that people would have a difficult time actually proving the harmlessness of other forms of speech, including "editorials criticizing government officials" and even religious sermons or feminist essays.[11]

A leading organization in challenging the wisdom of prosecuting obscenity and other "victimless crimes" is the Washington, D.C.-based Cato Institute, which espouses the libertarian philosophy of minimal government intrusion into people's private lives or business dealings. Cato's Adam Thierer writes, "Most adult entertainment [websites] allow consenting adults to enjoy sexually related materials without engaging in behavior that poses harm to others."[12] The original purpose of the unconstitutional Communications Decency Act was to protect children against pornography, and anti-pornography efforts are often promoted as designed to protect children from corrupting influence. The problem, notes Thierer, is that "In the name of 'protecting children,' policymakers oftentimes end up treating us all like juveniles."[13] Rather than criminalizing pornography to protect children, Thierer believes that a more sensible approach is to put the responsibility on parents to monitor, and restrict if necessary, their childrens' Internet usage. He writes:

> Parents must first purchase a computer, obtain an Internet access provider, set the system up, log on, and take a host of other steps before the Net is available to their children. If

parents have taken such steps to bring this technology into the home, they should not then expect regulators to assume the remainder of their parental obligations once the kids get online.[14]

Florida attorney Lawrence Walters, who represents webmasters of adult pornography sites, believes that the number one reason that obscenity laws have become obsolete is that "times have changed" since the wholesome era of the television show *Leave It to Beaver*, in which modern legal standards for obscenity were established. On his website, offering legal information and commentary, he writes that webmasters of sites featuring adult pornography "face draconian sanctions under puritanical obscenity laws, which have simply not recognized significant changes in societal attitudes toward erotic materials."[15] As evidence of pornography's societal acceptance, he points to the billions of dollars that adult videos and websites rake in each year. Philip Harvey, who operates a mail-order sex toy and erotica company, is more direct in his complaints, writing, "Americans are still living with the legacy of powerful leaders of the Christian church . . . who have persuaded generations of us to believe that all forms of sexual pleasure are sinful. . . . It is time we outlived their malevolent legacy."[16]

A global medium cannot be expected to meet local standards for every community.

In general, speech and other forms of expression such as photographs and movies are protected by the First Amendment. Like child pornography, so-called "obscenity" is not protected by the Constitution. The problem lies in deciding whether material is obscene, because not all pornography is obscene, and the legal standards established by the Supreme Court are confusing at best. In the landmark *Miller* v. *California* decision, the U.S. Supreme Court established a three-part test for determining whether material is "obscene" and therefore outside of the protection of the U.S. Constitution. That test involves the following three questions:

> (a) whether "the average person, applying contemporary community standards" would find that the work, taken as a whole, appeals to the prurient interest . . . (b) whether the work depicts or describes, in a patently offensive way, sexual conduct specifically defined by the applicable state law; and (c) whether the work, taken as a whole, lacks serious literary, artistic, political, or scientific value.[17]

FROM THE BENCH

Justices Express Doubt About Applying Local Standards to the Internet

Concurring

The economics and technology of Internet communication differ in important ways from those of telephones and mail. Paradoxically, as the District Court found, it is easy and cheap to reach a worldwide audience on the Internet but expensive if not impossible to reach a geographic subset. A Web publisher in a community where avant garde culture is the norm may have no desire to reach a national market; he may wish only to speak to his neighbors; nevertheless, if an eavesdropper in a more traditional, rural community chooses to listen in, there is nothing the publisher can do. As a practical matter, COPA [Child Online Protection Act] makes the eavesdropper the arbiter of propriety on the Web. And it is no answer to say that the speaker should "take the simple step of utilizing a [different] medium." Our prior decisions have voiced particular concern with laws that foreclose an entire medium of expression. ...[T]he danger they pose to the freedom of speech is readily apparent—by eliminating a common means of speaking, such measures can suppress too much speech.

[The] Court of Appeals ... may have been correct ... to conclude that in practical effect COPA imposes the most puritanical community standard on the entire country. We have observed that it is "neither realistic nor constitutionally sound to read the First Amendment as requiring that the people of Maine or Mississippi accept public depiction of conduct found tolerable in Las Vegas, or New York City." On the other hand, it is neither realistic nor beyond constitutional doubt for

The obvious problem with the test is that it involves a number of value judgments. Different people have a widely different understanding of the terms, "prurient interest," "patently offensive," and "serious value." Another problem is that community standards obviously differ from community to community. With older forms of pornography, such as movies and magazines, businesses could avoid liability by simply avoiding communities in which obscenity prosecutions were likely because of the communities' particularly conservative government officials and residents. The Internet does not allow websites to "pick and choose" their audiences in such a manner.

Congress, in effect, to impose the community standards of Maine or Mississippi on Las Vegas and New York. The national variation in community standards constitutes a particular burden on Internet speech.

Source: *Ashcroft* v. *ACLU,* No. 00-1293 (May 13, 2002; Kennedy, J., concurring in the judgment)

Dissenting

Appeals to prurient interests are commonplace on the Internet, as in older media. Many of those appeals lack serious value for minors as well as adults. Some are offensive to certain viewers but welcomed by others. For decades, our cases have recognized that the standards for judging their acceptability vary from viewer to viewer and from community to community. Those cases developed the requirement that communications should be protected if they do not violate contemporary community standards. In its original form, the community standard provided a shield for communications that are offensive only to the least tolerant members of society. Thus, the Court "has emphasized on more than one occasion that a principal concern in requiring that a judgment be made on the basis of 'contemporary community standards' is to assure that the material is judged neither on the basis of each juror's personal opinion, nor by its effect on a particularly sensitive or insensitive person or group." In the context of the Internet, however, community standards become a sword, rather than a shield. If a prurient appeal is offensive in a puritan village, it may be a crime to post it on the World Wide Web.

Source *Ashcroft* v. *ACLU,* No. 00-1293 (May 13, 2002; Stevens, J., dissenting)

Once a website is posted, it is available wherever an ISP makes the site available, and most ISPs in the United States do not limit subscribers' access to sites based on adult content.

> • **Could a community ban Internet Service Providers from providing service due to concerns over pornography?**

The Supreme Court considered the issue of how to apply community standards to the Internet when the ACLU challenged the constitutionality of the Child Online Protection Act (COPA). This federal law, using language that closely mirrors the *Miller* decision, prohibits posting obscene material on the Web for commercial purposes if the material is available to minors. In a splintered decision, the justices ruled that the fact that the law applied "community standards" to the Internet did not in itself render the law unconstitutional. The Supreme Court ruled, however, that the U.S. government could not enforce the law until a lower court determined whether other aspects of the law were unconstitutional. Writing separately, Justice John Paul Stevens criticized the idea of applying local standards to a global medium:

> In its original form, the community standard provided a shield for communications that are offensive only to the least tolerant members of society. Thus, the Court "has emphasized on more than one occasion that a principal concern in requiring that a judgment be made on the basis of 'contemporary community standards' is to assure that the material is judged neither on the basis of each juror's personal opinion, nor by its effect on a particularly sensitive or insensitive person or group. . . . In the context of the Internet, however, community standards become a sword, rather than a shield. If a prurient appeal is offensive in a puritan village, it may be a crime to post it on the World Wide Web.[18]

While the Supreme Court's decision focused on the question of whether the Internet should be forced to conform to local standards, some go so far as to question whether local community standards exist in today's world. Attorney Lawrence Walters argues that the globalization of the Internet and other forms of media, such as satellite and cable television, has created global standards for entertainment. He writes, "[It] is no longer possible for some small community to isolate itself in the attempt to claim that its value system somehow differs from the rest of the world's."[19]

Filtering software threatens legitimate speech.

With the Supreme Court taking a hard line against laws regulating the content of the Internet, lawmakers took a different approach to the issue. Rather than trying to limit the type of material that could be posted on the Internet, Congress turned its attention to filtering software, which blocks access to websites that contain prohibited words. Few people question whether parents should have the legal right to install filtering software on computers used by their children, although many people think that doing so is a bad idea, and numerous websites have offered advice on how to outwit popular filtering software.

Whether the government should be in the business of installing filtering software is another issue altogether and is certainly much more controversial. In 2000, Congress passed the Children's Internet Protection Act (CIPA), which strongly encouraged public libraries to install filtering software. Although the law did not directly require libraries to install filtering software on computers accessible to the public, libraries that refused to do so would no longer be eligible for federal funding under two key programs.

Librarians across the country reacted with outrage, not because they supported Internet pornography but because they opposed government censorship of information available in the library. Censorship is an especially touchy topic among librarians, given the vast numbers of literary works that have been censored over the years. Books such as Mark Twain's *The Adventures of Huckleberry Finn*, John Steinbeck's *Of Mice and Men*, and Alice Walker's *The Color Purple* have all been targets of frequent efforts to ban them from libraries.

Although some people were, in fact, using public library computers to access pornography, many librarians wanted to handle the problem internally. In fact, many libraries had already established their own Internet use policies, e.g., no playing computer games and no displaying websites containing erotica. Rather than allowing the government or the manufacturers of filtering

FROM THE BENCH

The Supreme Court Refuses to Treat the Internet Like Television and Radio

Neither before nor after the enactment of the [Communications Decency Act (CDA)] have the vast democratic fora of the Internet been subject to the type of government supervision and regulation that has attended the broadcast industry. Moreover, the Internet is not as "invasive" as radio or television. The District Court specifically found that "[c]ommunications over the Internet do not 'invade' an individual's home or appear on one's computer screen unbidden. Users seldom encounter content 'by accident.'" It also found that "[a]lmost all sexually explicit images are preceded by warnings as to the content," and cited testimony that "'odds are slim' that a user would come across a sexually explicit sight [*sic*] by accident."

Finally, unlike the conditions that prevailed when Congress first authorized regulation of the broadcast spectrum, the Internet can hardly be considered a "scarce" expressive commodity. It provides relatively unlimited, low cost capacity for communication of all kinds. The Government estimates that "[a]s many as 40 million people use the Internet today, and that figure is expected to grow to 200 million by 1999." This dynamic, multifaceted category of communication includes not only traditional print and news services, but also audio, video, and still images, as well as interactive, real time dialogue. Through the use of chat rooms, any person with a phone line can become a town crier with a voice that resonates farther than it could from any soapbox. Through the use of Web pages, mail exploders, and newsgroups, the same individual can become a pamphleteer. As the District Court found, "the content on the Internet is as diverse as human thought." We agree with its conclusion that our cases provide no basis for qualifying the level of First Amendment scrutiny that should be applied to this medium.

Source: *Reno* v. *ACLU 521* U.S. 844 (1997).

software to determine what information was fit for library research, many librarians wanted to continue to set their own policies.

- **Should librarians restrict what people can see on the Internet?**

After the passage of CIPA, the American Library Association (ALA), civil liberties groups, and individual librarians sued the federal government to prevent the law from taking effect. They argued that the law violated the First Amendment as an impermissible violation of free speech. The U.S. Supreme Court, however, upheld the law, issuing a splintered decision, in which none of the written opinions were backed by a majority of the nine justices. Four justices, led by Chief Justice Rehnquist, concluded:

> The [funding] programs were intended to help public libraries fulfill their traditional role of obtaining material of requisite and appropriate quality for educational and informational purposes. . . . [B]ecause public libraries have traditionally excluded pornographic material from their other collections, Congress could reasonably impose a parallel limitation on its Internet assistance programs. As the use of filtering software helps to carry out these programs, it is a permissible condition.[20]

Two other justices wrote separate opinions in which they said the law was saved by a provision of the law that allows adult library users to request that the filtering mechanism be turned off. It is unclear whether these justices would support a law calling for mandatory filtering without allowing adults to request that the filtering mechanism be disabled.

Although a disappointment to free-speech advocates, the ruling did not put the issue of Internet filtering completely to rest. The federal law in question does not require public libraries to use Internet filtering software. Public libraries remain free to allow unfiltered Internet access; however, libraries that do so lose out on some valuable funding from the federal government.

Therefore, one possible area of debate is whether local libraries should decide to go without federal funding. At the federal level, another area of debate is whether to extend the types of filtering requirements found in CIPA to universities that also receive federal funding. As the debate over the wisdom of using filtering software continues, many of the practical concerns raised by the American Library Association in challenging CIPA remain important, even if the Court has resolved the constitutional question in favor of allowing censorship.

In the aftermath of the *American Library Association* decision, states have considered passing laws requiring local libraries to install filtering software rather than giving up federal funding for their refusal to do so. Edward Johnson, Dean of Libraries at Oklahoma State University, criticized such a proposal as an assault on libraries' ability to provide "open access" that meets the needs of the communities they serve. He writes:

> Many public libraries have . . . chosen to install filtering software but others have not. Such local decision-making is preferable to legislation that would override a local governing body's legal authority and is compatible with Oklahoma's beliefs that the less government regulation the better.[21]

Like public libraries, universities receive a great deal of federal funding, both directly and indirectly. Direct means of support include grants supporting scientific, medical, and other types of academic research. Indirect support comes in the form of the substantial amount of money that the federal government devotes to student loans and academic scholarships. Although CIPA does not cover university libraries, as Douglas Archer noted in a publication of the University of Notre Dame's library system, "[T]here is nothing in theory to prevent Congress from attaching similar qualifications to federal funding legislation affecting academic libraries—especially in the current environment of heightened concern for security. . . ."[22]

One of the primary problems facing librarians who are forced to install filtering software is that they lose control over the types of information that they can offer to their patrons. Even librarians

FROM THE BENCH

The Supreme Court Rules That Even "Indecent" and "Patently Offensive" Material Deserves Constitutional Protection

The breadth of the CDA's coverage is wholly unprecedented [and] not limited to commercial speech or commercial entities. Its open-ended prohibitions embrace all nonprofit entities and individuals posting indecent messages or displaying them on their own computers in the presence of minors. The general, undefined terms "indecent" and "patently offensive" cover large amounts of nonpornographic material with serious educational or other value. Moreover, the "community standards" criterion as applied to the Internet means that any communication available to a nationwide audience will be judged by the standards of the community most likely to be offended by the message. The regulated subject matter includes any of the seven "dirty words" used in [a famous George Carlin] monologue, the use of which the government's expert acknowledged could constitute a felony. It may also extend to discussions about prison rape or safe sexual practices, artistic images that include nude subjects, and arguably the card catalogue of the Carnegie Library.

For the purposes of our decision, we need neither accept nor reject the government's submission that the First Amendment does not forbid a blanket prohibition on all "indecent" and "patently offensive" messages communicated to a 17-year-old—no matter how much value the message may contain and regardless of parental approval. It is at least clear that the strength of the government's interest in protecting minors is not equally strong throughout the coverage of this broad statute. Under the CDA, a parent allowing her 17-year-old to use the family computer to obtain information on the Internet that she, in her parental judgment, deems appropriate could face a lengthy prison term. Similarly, a parent who sent his 17-year-old college freshman information on birth control via e-mail could be incarcerated even though neither he, his child, nor anyone in their home community, found the material "indecent" or "patently offensive," if the college town's community thought otherwise.

Source: *Reno* v. *ACLU 421* U.S. 844 (1997)

who agree that patrons should not be using a computer to access pornography fear that if a line is drawn—by the government or by software manufacturers—between what is "acceptable" and what is not acceptable, then literary works and health information will be blocked. As the ALA argued in its lawsuit:

> A library that installs blocking software . . . has no way of knowing which sites will be blocked. The filter companies consider their control lists to be proprietary, and customers are not allowed to access them. . . . As a result, the only way for a library administrator to know whether a particular site will be blocked is through individual trial and error.[23]

What one person considers offensive might not be considered offensive by most people, and when filtering companies make decisions in secret, many fear that too much material is being censored.

In fact, the ALA has cited "overblocking" as one of its biggest concerns with filtering software. Many librarians believe that people use libraries for legitimate research on topics that some people find offensive. For example, people might be searching for information about sexually transmitted diseases. The ALA argued that some might consider the operation of filtering software as a form of discrimination, stating, "Especially pernicious is blocking software's disproportionate effect on sites dealing with sensitive sexual issues, such as sexual health and gay and lesbian sites."[24] The brief cited a study showing that about 10 percent of websites containing sexual health information were blocked by filtering software.

In addition to questionable decisions being made about whether certain material is inappropriate, the manner in which the software operates could lead to further censorship of valuable material. When the filtering company identifies material deemed inappropriate, the software does not block only those pages containing that specific material. Instead, the ALA noted,

"If a site with hundreds of pages includes even a few pages that ostensibly meet the filtering company's content categories, the company will block the entire site,"[25] a solution that the organization called "overbroad."

Worse yet, the ALA noted, some filtering programs, upon discovering pages containing inappropriate material, will block other websites. Placing material on the Web requires a server, or computer accessible to Internet users. Typically, servers are large computers with high-speed connections, and purchasing and maintaining a server is very expensive. Therefore, many individuals, small businesses, clubs, and non-profit organizations do not own their own servers, instead renting server space or using a free website hosting service. As a result, many servers host multiple websites, and even though the websites are created by different people for different purposes, the fact that they share the same server can lead filtering programs to block all of the sites. As a result, writes librarian Douglas Archer:

> [If] a law firm, a baker, a florist, an artist, a soccer league and an erotic photographer or pornographer (depending on your tastes and definition) all buy space on a local internet service provider's server . . . the fact that the erotica/pornography site is getting frequent hits may cause everyone on the server to be blocked.[26]

Summary

Although the Supreme Court has stricken down broad restrictions on the type of material that can be posted on the Internet, Congress and prosecutors continue to target people who post sexually explicit material. Many civil libertarians believe that efforts to keep pornography out of children's hands threaten free speech for everyone.

"Cleaning up" the Internet Protects Its Usefulness

During the 1990s, an increasing number of households signed up for Internet access, but many households still were not "wired." For many people, the public library remained the only place to surf the Web. Libraries offered Internet access primarily because the wealth of information available online aided their mission of providing information to the public. The Internet, however, was also growing as a source of amusement—some innocent, some not so innocent. Many people found enjoyment in joining discussions in chat rooms, shopping online, following their favorite sports teams, listening to music, and buying and selling on E-bay. Others were drawn to the Internet primarily for its enormous cache of pornography, including illegal child pornography.

When the public library system in Greenville, South Carolina, first began offering public Internet access in 1998, librarians had high hopes that the Internet terminals would open up new worlds to their patrons. Many people were indeed being exposed to new worlds, but too often the experience was a case of indecent exposure. Librarians recorded incidents of people watching graphic videos over the Internet, including depictions of men engaged in sex acts with young boys and men and women engaged in sex acts with animals. In several cases, adults showed the pornography to children using the library.

The Greenville librarians felt that they had to do something to stem the tide of pornography, so they started confronting people using computers to view pornography and installed "privacy desks" to shield others from inadvertently viewing the offending material. These measures, however, did not work, and at least one in five websites visited by library patrons were pornography sites. Ultimately, the library decided to install filtering software on the computers available to the public, which blocked the use of search engines to retrieve pornography and blocked known pornography sites. The installation of the filtering software stopped the flood of complaints from angry parents and library users unwillingly exposed to pornography.

The Greenville library applauded the Supreme Court's decision in the *U.S. v. American Library Association*, which upheld a federal law requiring public libraries to install filtering software in order to qualify for federal funding under two specific programs. In many ways, the debate over library filtering is a small-scale version of the debate about regulating the content of the Internet. Many of the same arguments about harm to minors and diminishing the research and communicative value of the Internet are made when justifying attempts to restrict the availability of offensive material online. Many conservative politicians, religious groups, concerned parents, and others believe that the government should more actively combat the growing tide of pornography available on the Internet and that communities should be allowed to protect their children from offensive materials, even if they are delivered by new technology. In the meantime, the debate over library filtering continues as libraries decide whether to install filtering software or reject federal funding.

Law enforcement officials must stem the tide of obscenity on the Internet.

During the latter half of the 1990s and the early years of the twenty-first century, as the popularity of the Internet exploded, federal prosecutors focused their anti-pornography efforts almost exclusively on halting child pornography on the theory that children are victimized by the making of child pornography. Many conservatives and feminists, however, also reject the idea that pornography featuring adult models is a "victimless crime." Under conservative Attorney General John Ashcroft, the U.S. Department of Justice has renewed efforts to prosecute purveyors of adult pornography.

The Reverand Donald Wildmon, one of the nation's most prominent anti-pornography crusaders, flatly rejects the idea that pornography is a "victimless crime." In his book, *The Case Against Pornography*, Wildmon discusses the case of David Eugene Pyles, who was convicted of rape and attempted murder for a brutal attack on a 17-year-old. Claiming that "Pornography affects not only minds already perverted, but it can pervert minds,"[27] Wildmon writes that Pyles' crime was inspired by pornography. Citing Pyles' "virtually spotless past" as an army veteran and family man, Wildmon blames Pyles' "diet of perversion"—including nude magazine photos, novels describing brutal sex acts, and sexually violent movies—for leading him to commit the attack. Wildmon concludes that the victim of the attack "and thousands upon thousands of other people" are the victims of pornography. "For Wildmon, it is not just the victims of sexual assaults who are the victims of pornography. "Very clearly, we are *all* victims," he writes.[28]

> • If most rapists use pornography, does that information support the conclusion that using pornography causes people to commit rapes? What if it was determined that most rapists smoke cigarettes?

The conservative group Citizens for Community Values has declared May to be "Victims of Pornography Awareness Month." Among the victims listed on the group's website are women who are exploited for profit by the pornography industry, young people whose innocence is destroyed by viewing pornography, the wives of men addicted to pornography, and pornography addicts themselves. Ultimately, the group claims, pornography harms everyone because "society . . . has become desensitized and dependent upon sex-charged images."[29]

Objections to pornography are not limited to conservatives. Many otherwise liberal feminists believe that pornography is harmful to women as a group because the widespread availability of pornography to men encourages the development of sexist and abusive attitudes toward women. Feminist Andrea Dworkin blames pornography for "the active subordination of women: the creation of a sexual dynamic in which the putting-down of women, the suppression of women, and ultimately the brutalization of women, *is* what sex is taken to be."[30]

Although people with liberal political philosophies typically support broad protections of free speech, some feminists reject the idea that protecting pornography protects free speech. Noted University of Michigan law professor Catherine A. MacKinnon writes that rather than encouraging freedom of thought, pornography "enslaves women's minds and bodies inseparably." Because of the disrespectful view of women advanced by pornography, she concludes, "the free speech of men silences the free speech of women."[31]

The backlash against pornography is gaining momentum against legislators. Republican Congressman Tom Osborne of Nebraska agrees that pornography cannot be described accurately as a "victimless crime" and has urged his colleagues to act. Noting that "80 to 90 percent of pedophiles and rapists report using pornography, oft times before they commit an event,"[32] Osborne has compared pornography to advertising for criminal acts, saying:

> So, some people say, well, what is the big deal? Pornography is harmless. It does not really have any victim. Yet, if you think about it, we spend billions of dollars in this country on commercials, and if those commercials did not change behavior, if what you see and what you hear and what you read does not change your behavior, then we are spending billions of dollars unnecessarily. So, obviously, the pornography industry does have a tremendous impact on behavior and the environments that our young people exist in.[33]

A local community must be able to uphold its standards, regardless of the medium.

Undeniably, the Internet is a global medium. The operators of pornographic websites are able to market their products worldwide, instantly and inexpensively. When a person visits a pornographic website, it is difficult, if not impossible, for the operator of the site to verify where the person lives. Some have used this set of circumstances to argue that operators of pornographic websites should not be subjected to local standards of decency because they cannot control where their products are being viewed. Supporters of anti-pornography laws counter that communities must be able to uphold their local standards, regardless of the medium.

Although it might be easier for movie theaters and bookstores than it is for website operators to ensure that their products meet local standards, supporters of anti-pornography laws say that difficulty in complying with the law should not excuse people from having to comply with the law. In other words, communities should not lose the power they hold to control the showing of pornographic movies or the sale of pornographic magazines. Defending the Child Online Protection Act (COPA), a law requiring pornographic websites to restrict access to material deemed by community standards to be harmful to minors, the conservative American Center for

FROM THE BENCH

Justice Thomas Believes That Local Standards Must Be Respected

The Court of Appeals below concluded that [cases upholding restrictions on mail-order pornography and phone sex] "are easily distinguished from the present case" because in both of those cases "the defendants had the ability to control the distribution of controversial material with respect to the geographic communities into which they released it" whereas "Web publishers have no such comparable control." In neither [case], however, was the speaker's ability to target the release of material into particular geographic areas integral to the legal analysis....If a publisher chooses to send its material into a particular community, this Court's jurisprudence teaches that it is the publisher's responsibility to abide by that community's standards. The publisher's burden does not change simply because it decides to distribute its material to every community in the Nation. Nor does it change because the publisher may wish to speak only to those in a "community where avant garde culture is the norm" but nonetheless utilizes a medium that transmits its speech from coast to coast. If a publisher wishes for its material to be judged only by the standards of particular communities, then it need only take the simple step of utilizing a medium that enables it to target the release of its material into those communities.

Source: *Ashcroft* v. *ACLU*, No. 00-1293 (May 13, 2002; opinion of Thomas, J.)

Law and Justice compared COPA to laws "obliging commercial vendors to place 'harmful to minors' material behind a 'blinder rack,' in a 'sealed wrapper,' or inside an 'opaque cover,' and [requiring] proof of adult status for purchase of such materials." [34]

> • **Who should bear the burden of restricting children's access to pornography—parents or the operators of websites?**

In a case in which the Supreme Court ruled that the federal government could not enforce COPA, several justices nevertheless accepted the idea that pornographers cannot escape local standards just because the Internet is a global medium. Joined by two other justices, Clarence Thomas noted that while the law required website operators to conform to local standards of decency, the law contained an exception for material of "serious literary, artistic, political, or scientific value," a judgment not subject to local community standards. Rather, he wrote, "[The] serious value requirement . . . allows appellate courts to impose some limitations and regularity on the definition by setting, as a matter of law, a national floor for socially redeeming value." [35] In these justices' opinion, as long as federal courts could uphold First Amendment free speech rights by protecting materials of serious value, no harm could result from allowing communities to set their own standards for what is offensive.

Filtering software is a reasonable solution to a serious problem.

In *U.S. v. American Library Association*, the U.S. Supreme Court upheld the constitutionality of a federal law—the Children's Internet Protection Act (CIPA), not to be confused with COPA—requiring public libraries to install filtering software in exchange for receiving federal funding under two specific programs. Given that public libraries receive only a small portion of their funding through these federal programs, however, the debate over library Internet filtering continued. Some states, including Utah, passed state laws mandating that libraries install the filtering software.

Although the American Library Association (ALA) and many individual librarians have opposed filtering software as an abridgement of the freedom to conduct research, other librarians reject the argument. Although they agree with the ALA that the Internet is a valuable research tool, they believe that the installation of filtering software makes the Internet more valuable to the community as a research tool.

THE LETTER OF THE LAW

Child Online Protection Act (COPA)

So far, courts have blocked the federal government from enforcing this law.

Whoever knowingly and with knowledge of the character of the material, in interstate or foreign commerce by means of the World Wide Web, makes any communication for commercial purposes that is available to any minor and that includes any material that is harmful to minors shall be fined not more than $50,000, imprisoned not more than 6 months, or both.

The term "material that is harmful to minors" means any communication, picture, image, graphic image file, article, recording, writing, or other matter of any kind that is obscene or that

A) the average person, applying contemporary community standards, would find, taking the material as a whole and with respect to minors, is designed to appeal to, or is designed to pander to, the prurient interest;

B) depicts, describes, or represents, in a manner patently offensive with respect to minors, an actual or simulated sexual act or sexual contact, an actual or simulated normal or perverted sexual act, or a lewd exhibition of the genitals or post-pubescent female breast; and

C) taken as a whole, lacks serious literary, artistic, political, or scientific value for minors.

In a brief submitted to the Supreme Court in the *ALA* case, three public libraries argued that librarians should be free to use filtering software because it is a librarian's role to

---

FROM THE BENCH

Supreme Court: Requiring Libraries to Use Filtering Software Is Constitutional

The District Court [ruled that] whereas a library reviews and affirmatively chooses to acquire every book in its collection, it does not review every Website that it makes available. Based on this distinction, the court reasoned that a public library enjoys less discretion in deciding which Internet materials to make available than in making book selections. We do not find this distinction constitutionally relevant. A library's failure to make quality-based judgments about all the material it furnishes from the Web does not somehow taint the judgments it does make. A library's need to exercise judgment in making collection decisions depends on its traditional role in identifying suitable and worthwhile material; it is no less entitled to play that role when it collects material from the Internet than when it collects material from any other source. Most libraries already exclude pornography from their print collections because they deem it inappropriate for inclusion. We do not subject these decisions to heightened scrutiny; it would make little sense to treat libraries' judgments to block online pornography any differently, when these judgments are made for just the same reason.

Moreover, because of the vast quantity of material on the Internet and the rapid pace at which it changes, libraries cannot possibly segregate, item by item, all the Internet material that is appropriate for inclusion from all that is not. While a library could limit its Internet collection to just those sites it found worthwhile, it could do so only at the cost of excluding an enormous amount of valuable information that it lacks the capacity to review. Given that tradeoff, it is entirely reasonable for public libraries to reject that approach and instead exclude certain categories of content, without making individualized judgments that everything they do make available has requisite and appropriate quality.

Source: *U.S. v. American Library Association*, No. 02-361 (June 23, 2003; opinion of Rehnquist, J.)

determine the types of material that are available in the library. The brief stated:

> [M]any public libraries think they should be free to select books without being subject to judicial review[, and] . . . that this "freedom to choose" also applies to the Internet and a decision to install filtering software. . . . The task of every library is to select material, based on its content, which will be made available to the library patrons. . . . [The] Internet contains an extensive amount of illegal obscenity and child pornography, unfiltered access to the Internet will inevitably allow library patrons to display unprotected and illegal materials in a public place.[36]

The biggest concern of many librarians, and of Congress in passing CIPA, was that children were being exposed to pornography in public libraries, either by accessing it themselves or by inadvertently viewing pornography retrieved by other patrons. Defending filtering laws on the NPR radio program *Justice Talking*, attorney Bruce Taylor said that filtering software is necessary to "make this Internet something that children can turn on in the home, in the school, in their library . . . [and search for terms like] *boys, girls, toys, boy scouts, actresses*, or *cheerleader* and not get a hundred hot links to hard-core porn sites."[37] When Taylor made those comments, he was an attorney for the conservative National Law Center for Children and Families, but he was later appointed a federal prosecutor and vowed to enforce anti-pornography laws more vigorously.

• **Could the federal government deny funding to libraries that refuse to hang a sign reading, "Vote Republican" or "Vote Democrat"?**

Although the primary goal of CIPA is to protect children from viewing inappropriate material, some people have argued that similar requirements should be imposed upon university libraries, even though they primarily serve adults. At Southern Utah University, two professors proposed a university-wide computer policy that would forbid students, faculty, and staff from using university computers or network connections to access "sexually explicit material" defined as depictions of sex acts and nudity.[38] Under the proposed policy, anyone wishing to access such materials for academic research purposes would be required to receive advance permission from the head of an academic department and two high-ranking university officials.[38]

The professors thought that the policy would help to further the university's mission as a place of higher learning. By limiting the use of computers for accessing pornography, they reasoned, more resources would be available for legitimate academic study. While acknowledging that, "[on] a university campus, freedom of inquiry, or academic freedom, is necessary as a generalized right," the professors' proposed policy also argued that "academic freedom must end where moral impropriety begins."[39]

THE LETTER OF THE LAW

Children's Internet Protection Act (CIPA)

No funds may be used to purchase computers used to access the Internet, or to pay for direct costs associated with accessing the Internet, for such library unless such library (i) has in place a policy of Internet safety for minors that includes the operation of a technology protection measure with respect to any of its computers with Internet access that protects against access through such computers to visual depictions that are

(I) obscene;

(II) child pornography; or

(III) harmful to minors . . .

The Supreme Court upheld this law in U.S. v. American Library Association. The definition of "harmful to minors" is identical to that used in the Child Online Protection Act (COPA).

The professors' argument relied on the premise that library computers are a scarce resource and that they therefore should be reserved for serious research purposes. The conservative American Center for Law and Justice made a similar argument in the *ALA* case, noting that libraries frequently ensure the availability of computer terminals by prohibiting patrons from playing video games or checking e-mail. The group argued that in the same way libraries "routinely [bar] patrons from using library computers with Internet access for entertainment, interpersonal communication, [and] shopping," they should also be able to bar "the indulgence of prurient interests."[40]

Summary

The Supreme Court has acknowledged that free speech has its limits and that some restrictions on free speech are necessary to protect other rights. Opponents of Internet pornography believe that strong restrictions are needed to protect the victims of pornography—both adults and children—and that the global nature of the Internet should not be used as an excuse for trampling on community standards of decency.

File Sharing Is an Important Technology That Helps Artists and Promotes Creativity

DJ Xealot, a tech-savvy disc jockey who recorded and remixed techno and dance tracks, saw the Internet as a way of making it big. He posted several of his songs on MP3.com, a website allowing visitors to download songs in the popular MP3 file format for a fee. DJ Xealot made a little money by doing this, but in November 1999, he found a way to promote his music much more effectively. He made his songs available on Napster, a "song-swapping" service that allowed users to download songs from other people's computers for free while making the users' own song libraries available to others. As the service grew in popularity, people could download thousands of songs without ever having to pay for them as they would on MP3.com.

Although it seems strange to think that giving something away would be a good way of making money, DJ Xealot's income shot up after making his songs available on Napster. He attached an electronic "tag" to his songs that pointed listeners to his website where they could purchase his CDs or pay to download additional songs. The money that he earned selling CDs and downloads helped to pay for his college tuition at the University of Florida. He also received a great deal of publicity that helped further his career as a musician and graphic artist. In his words, "Napster is a great promotion tool that provides an affordable alternative to major [recording] labels for artists like myself."[41]

Napster was an example of a peer-to-peer, or "P2P" network, which operates in a manner different from the World Wide Web. For an Internet connection to happen, one computer must act as the "server" or the computer that transmits information, and another acts as the "client" or the computer that receives information. When a computer user connects to the World Wide Web and visits a website like E-bay or Amazon.com, he or she is accessing information from a powerful server capable of storing and transmitting a great deal of information. These computers are very fast and are "dedicated servers," meaning that they are always on (unless some type of problem shuts them down). By contrast, when someone logs on to a P2P network, his or her computer acts not only as a client that can retrieve information from other computers but also as a server that can transmit information to other computers. Because the computers have equal roles, they are considered "peers," much like classmates in school.

> • **Should artists be able to control the distribution of their music for promotional purposes?**

By far the most popular use of P2P networks has been sharing music files as was done on Napster at the time. A Napster user would log into the network, check the main directory of songs, and find someone who had a particular song stored on his or her computer. At the same time someone was searching for a song, someone else could be copying a song from his or her computer. At the time DJ Xealot's career began to take off,

Napster was an incredibly popular service, but it was operating at the fringes of the law.

For many people, Napster provided a great way to download a lot of free music, and for some artists, like DJ Xealot, a great way of promoting their careers. However, Napster and its many users did not have permission to share many of the songs that were being shared, and in the United States, copyright law protects creations such as songs, books, poems, and photographs. The person who creates the work has the right to charge people who use or copy his or her creation, and also has the right to prevent other people from using the work. The protection of "intellectual property," such as copyrights and patents on inventions, is granted by federal law and has its basis in the Constitution, which provides: "The Congress shall have power to . . . promote the progress of science and useful arts, by securing for limited times to authors and inventors the exclusive right to their respective writings and discoveries. . . ."[42] Federal law allows a copyright to be assigned (sold or given) to another person or company, such as a record label or publishing house.

Many songwriters, musicians, and recording companies did not share DJ Xealot's positive opinion of Napster and sued the company to shut down its file-sharing service. They alleged that Napster was violating federal copyright law and that by enabling free downloads, Napster was denying them the right to profit from their own creations. They argued that Napster encouraged the illegal sharing of files on its network by distributing its file-sharing software and by operating a central server that contained a directory of songs that were available for sharing. In the spring of 2001, a federal court agreed that Napster's failure to prevent the sharing of copyrighted music files violated federal copyright law and ordered that Napster be shut down. Although Napster later reemerged as a paid service selling licensed copies of music, its days as a free file-sharing service were over.

Even before Napster was shut down, other file-sharing services had already popped up, and Napster's demise led to a boom in their popularity. New services, such as KaZaA, Grokster, and Morpheus, operated differently from Napster. Unlike Napster, which operated a central server, these new networks were "true" peer-to-peer networks in that the company merely distributed the software, and then had no further involvement in the file sharing. All searching and file transferring were done from one home computer to another. A federal judge handed the recording industry a major setback in 2003 when he ruled that software companies StreamCast and Grokster could not be held liable for copyright infringement committed with their Morpheus and Grokster programs. He ruled:

> Neither StreamCast nor Grokster facilitates the exchange of files between users in the way Napster did. Users connect to the respective networks, select which files to share, send and receive searches, and download files, all with no material involvement of Defendants. If either Defendant closed their doors and deactivated all computers within their control, users of their products could continue sharing files with little or no interruption.[43]

Although the recording industry appealed the decision and vowed to continue fighting the makers of file-sharing software in both the courts and in Congress, the industry also reverted to "Plan B." Because the court ruled that individual users, rather than the software companies, were responsible for the copyright infringement, the recording industry, through its trade association the Recording Industry Association of America (RIAA), began a series of lawsuits against "everyday" people who used services such as KaZaA, Grokster, and Morpheus.

P2P networks have many legitimate uses.

The recording industry's decision to start suing home computer users has sparked not only nervousness but quite a bit of outrage. The image of a large multinational corporation suing teenagers and their parents strikes many people as ugly corporate greed. Not only have many people rushed to the defense of individual song swappers, they have also come to the defense of peer-to-peer technology because they do not want new networks such as KaZaA and Morpheus to fall to the same fate as the original Napster network. Fighting against efforts to shut down these services in the courts and legislators, proponents have pointed to the many uses that P2P networks have other than trading copyrighted music files.

Public Knowledge is a Washington, D.C.-based organization that favors less restrictive copyright laws in order to encourage the exchange of ideas and information over the Internet. Although the group has criticized the RIAA's lawsuits against individual song swappers, it acknowledges that people face liability under current copyright laws for making copyrighted songs available on P2P networks. In an effort to stem legislation that would further restrict P2P networks, the organization's executive director testified to Congress that P2P networks hold great potential for academic studies. She gave the following example:

> Robert Kirkpatrick, Distinguished Associate Professor of English and Director of the London Summer Honors Program at the University of North Carolina at Chapel Hill, used Groove Network's P2P tools to manage a class in the composition of poetry. Among other things, Kirkpatrick used P2P technology to encourage collaborative editing and comment on students' work, adjust the syllabus, archive course materials, and create a list of links to resources of poetic forms and vast archives of complete works of poems and critical writing. The class also uses the Groove tools for a class forum and an announcement board to share information on musical, dramatic and other events on campus. Kirkpatrick said that P2P technology "makes it possible to extend that most expensive form of education— one-on-one tutorial—into a cohesive class experience. . . . It comes very close to being, for me, the ideal academic tool." [44]

The fact that P2P networks have many legitimate uses has a legal significance because the Supreme Court has stated that a technology that allows copying materials is lawful so long as it is "capable of substantial non-infringing uses."[45] This standard, which has allowed the continuing sale of photocopiers and the development of new technologies such as compact disc (CD) burners, was developed in an early case about the legality of video

FROM THE BENCH

Judge Rules That Grokster and Morpheus P2P Software Has Legitimate Uses

In *Sony Corp. of America* v. *Universal City Studios, Inc.*, the sale of video cassette recorders ("VCR"s) did not subject Sony to contributory copyright liability, even though Sony knew as a general matter that the machines could be used, and were being used, to infringe the plaintiffs' copyrighted works. Because video tape recorders were capable of both infringing and "substantial noninfringing uses," generic or "constructive" knowledge of infringing activity was insufficient to warrant liability based on the mere retail of Sony's products. "[T]he sale of copying equipment, like the sale of other articles of commerce, does not constitute contributory infringement" if the product is "capable of substantial non-infringing uses."

Here, it is undisputed that there are substantial non-infringing uses for Defendants' software—e.g., distributing movie trailers, free songs, or other noncopyrighted works; using the software in countries where it is legal; or sharing the works of Shakespeare. For instance, StreamCast has adduced evidence that the Morpheus program is regularly used to facilitate and search for public domain materials, government documents, media content for which distribution is authorized, media content as to which the rights owners do not object to distribution, and computer software for which distribution is permitted. The same is true of Grokster's software… [such as] Grokster's partnership with GigAmerica, a company which claimed to host music from 6,000 independent bands and musicians as of May 2002.

Furthermore, as the Supreme Court has explained, the existence of substantial noninfringing uses turns not only on a product's current uses, but also on potential future noninfringing uses. Plaintiffs do not dispute that Defendants' software is being used, and could be used, for substantial noninfringing purposes.

Source: *Metro-Goldwyn Mayer Studios, Inc.* v. *Grokster, Ltd.*, No. CV01-08541 (C.D. Cal. 2003)

cassette recorders (VCRs). In 1984, as the popularity of VCRs was growing rapidly, the Supreme Court considered a lawsuit by a Universal City Studios against Sony, which manufactured the Betamax, a popular brand of VCR. The movie studio wanted to force Sony to stop making VCRs capable of recording the studio's movies because Universal believed that videotaping movies threatened its ability to profit from its movies. Although it is true that VCRs could be used to make pirated copies of videotapes for sale, VCRs are also widely used to videotape shows for viewing in a private home for the user's convenience.

The Court rejected Universal Studio's claim that recording movies for home use was a violation of the copyright law and therefore refused to hold Sony responsible for "contributory infringement" or helping people skirt the copyright laws. The Court concluded:

> First, Sony demonstrated a significant likelihood that substantial numbers of copyright holders who license their works for broadcast on free television would not object to having their broadcasts time-shifted by private viewers. And second, respondents failed to demonstrate that time-shifting would cause any likelihood of non-minimal harm to the potential market for, or the value of, their copyrighted works. The Betamax is, therefore, capable of substantial non-infringing uses. Sony's sale of such equipment to the general public does not constitute contributory infringement of respondents' copyrights.[46]

At the time of the decision, home videotaping was still relatively new, and the Court used the somewhat awkward term "time-shifting" to describe the now common practice of recording a show to watch it later. Such practices, however, are commonly regarded as a type of "fair use" of copyrighted material. Although copyright law generally prohibits copying materials protected by copyright, an exception is made for "fair use," which is determined based upon a number of factors, including whether the copy made is for private use or for sale and whether the copying is done for educational reasons.

Copying songs is harmless and might even be helpful.

For many people, song swapping is itself a legitimate use of P2P networks. Despite what some courts have said, these people continue to believe that sharing copyrighted music and other materials online is permissible so long as it is not done for a profit. They compare song swapping to other activities that involve the copying of copyrighted material but fall within the bounds of copyright law. Some common examples include videotaping a television show to watch later or making a backup copy of a computer program to protect against crashes. A September 2003 Harris Interactive Poll concluded that 75 percent of Americans believe that while downloading copyrighted material and then selling it should be illegal, downloading copyrighted music for personal use is an "innocent act" that should be allowed. The same poll also concluded that 70 percent of Americans think that if CD prices were lower, people would download a lot less music.[47]

* **Have you ever swapped songs on line? Do you feel like you violated the law?**

Some people have continued to argue that song swapping is a "fair use" of copyrighted material. Facing a lawsuit after his two teenage daughters downloaded and shared hundreds of songs using KaZaA, a California man claimed that his daughters' use of KaZaA for copying and sharing music was an example of fair use because enjoying and listening to music has educational value. In court documents responding to the industry's lawsuit, he argued:

> Any copying or usage of music by Defendant or members of his family or household was done strictly for personal use or nonprofit educational, scholarship, research, criticism or comment purposes put to productive use in studying music and

performance styles as an adjunct to school music classes. . . . The method of sharing music files from the website www.KaZaA.com was freely discussed by teachers and students in schools attended by members of the Defendant's household, universally practiced by schoolmates of said household members, and resulting recordings were openly utilized in school classes attended by said household members. The practice of sharing files through the KaZaA website was thus for the sake of broadening the students' and teachers' understanding of the musical subject matter, and was thus for a socially beneficial and widely accepted purpose.[48]

He further supported his claim of fair use by arguing that just as home videotaping did not threaten the business of the movie industry, song swapping did not threaten the business of

THE LETTER OF THE LAW

Fair Use of Copyrighted Material

[The] fair use of a copyrighted work, including such use by reproduction in copies or phonorecords or by any other means specified by that section, for purposes such as criticism, comment, news reporting, teaching (including multiple copies for classroom use), scholarship, or research, is not an infringement of copyright. In determining whether the use made of a work in any particular case is a fair use the factors to be considered shall include

(1) the purpose and character of the use, including whether such use is of a commercial nature or is for nonprofit educational purposes;

(2) the nature of the copyrighted work;

(3) the amount and substantiality of the portion used in relation to the copyrighted work as a whole; and

(4) the effect of the use upon the potential market for or value of the copyrighted work.

Source: 17 U.S.C. § 107

the recording industry and was therefore a noncommercial fair use. The documents alleged:

> The recordings obtained by said students' file sharing from the KaZaA website could not have been for any commercial purposes: indeed, during all relevant times, said students, including members of Defendant's household, continued to buy substantial quantities of CDs manufactured and sold by Plaintiffs at high retail prices. Thus any file sharing by said household members had no adverse effect on the potential market for or value of its copyrighted works. . . . Any file sharing of songs through the website www.KaZaA.com by Defendant or members of Defendant's household was for nonprofit educational purposes, and thus under the protection of the Fair Use Doctrine set forth in Section 107 of the Copyright Act. . . .[49]

• **Can song swapping really be called an educational pursuit?**

During the Napster lawsuit, Napster had commissioned a report by Stanford University economist Robert Hall, who noted that CD sales had grown even after Napster became available:

> National unit sales at retail of CDs for the first quarter of 1999 (prior to the public release of Napster, in August 1999) . . . were 164 million—a 3.3 percent increase over unit sales in the first quarter of 1998. After the appearance of Napster, unit sales in the first quarter of 2000 rose to 175 million—a growth rate of 6.7 percent over the same period in 1999. This growth exceeds the growth of sales of goods and services in general in the U.S. economy.[50]

Based on information about CD sales, Hall's report went so far as to conclude that song swapping actually helped the recording industry boost its sales. He stated: "[These] data are consistent with the view that the favorable effects of higher volumes of exchange activities outweigh the adverse effects. For example, Napster and other methods of exchanging digital music may expose large numbers of new listeners to various artists' work, resulting in higher CD sales."

Many artists agree with Hall's conclusion and encourage fans to swap music on P2P networks. Rapper Chuck D of Public Enemy submitted a declaration in connection with the Napster lawsuit, stating his belief that the high costs of recording, shipping, and promoting an album through traditional channels hurt the vast majority of musicians by allowing only a handful of artists selected by the recording industry to become successful. He explained:

> Based on my extensive involvement in the music industry and the Internet, I know that the Internet in general, and Napster in particular, allow artists to expose and promote themselves to the global community of music lovers without relying on the big, corporate recording labels. Having been connected to the genre of hip hop and rap music for 22 years, I have witnessed the lack of support provided by the Plaintiff record companies to the majority of artists, song writers, producers and labels as they seek to reach their fan base. With radio choosing the more traditional, popular favorites, and the prohibitive expense of video production and other promotional devices, getting a record to the fans is extremely difficult and expensive. Napster and its "distributed aggregation" model for use of the Internet represent a valuable alternative to having artists rely on the large recording companies to select, record, promote, and sell their music. . . . [51]

The rapper, who has also started several Internet music ventures, noted that the recording industry put up the costs of recording and promoting an album but then recouped these costs by deducting them from the royalties that they paid to artists. He explained: "The label charges the cost of the CD and [promotional expenses] against the artist's royalties, even though the artist may be earning royalties of only a few cents on the dollar. By this practice, an artist who sells a million units may yet receive no royalties and still be considered 'unrecouped.'"[52]

Chuck D believes that the lower costs of Internet song swapping present opportunities for artists and songwriters to control a greater share of the income that their music generates. Calling the system of recouping royalties "digital sharecropping"—a reference to farmers who worked other people's land primarily for the owners' profit—he characterized song swapping as a way for more people to earn their living as musicians:

> "Peer-to-peer" trading operates as massive "word of mouth," or "word of mouse" promotion. And artists can hold on to the composition, performance *and* recording rights of their music and thus increase the amount of revenue directed to the artist per recording sold. In this way, artists can make a good living selling a modest number of recordings, and the musical career can belong to more artists, not just the handful of acts that the major labels decide to promote.[53]

The recording industry has not taken advantage of Internet technology.

Sharing electronic music files on a peer-to-peer network is a much different way of bringing music into people's homes than the traditional method of selling CDs (and before that, tapes and records). Manufacturing and shipping CDs requires money, and running a retail music store also costs money. As Chuck D noted in his declaration in the Napster case, a great deal of money is spent on promoting music as well. Economists call the many costs involved in bringing a product from its creator (in this case, the musician) to the buyer "transaction costs." In the traditional way of doing business, musical recordings had high transaction costs that made purchasing music relatively expensive. By contrast, the quick electronic transfer of music files and the promotion of music by word of mouth from Internet user to Internet user makes transaction costs minimal.

While acknowledging that online distribution of music poses a huge threat to recording companies, proponents of peer-to-peer networking believe that this threat is good for business because lowering transaction costs means that more people are able to get what they want. Some people believe that the music industry should abandon its traditional way of doing business and shift its attention from stopping file sharing to figuring out a new business plan that would allow them to make money from the Internet.

In an amicus brief in the *Napster* case, the conservative Eagle Forum and the Association of American Physicians and Surgeons argued that file sharing helped the economy, stating:

> Economically, it is not desirable or feasible to block inno-
> vations that, like the Napster innovation here, eliminate
> substantial transaction costs of distribution. As outdated
> methods of distributing information are supplemented by
> more efficient directory-based non-commercial distribution,
> the resultant reduction in transaction cost promotes more
> music creation. The Internet is, above all, an eliminator of
> costs of distribution that burden the economy, and Nobel
> laureate economist Ronald Coase proved that an optimized
> economy results from a no-transaction-cost system. Just as
> our overall economy is lifted by the internet, the creation and
> consumption of music is lifted by non-commercial internet
> sharing as well.[54]

The groups also argued that Napster harmed—if anyone— only the record companies, and that this harm was their own fault: While recording companies had the opportunity to profit from the Internet, those companies that did not adapt to tech- nological advances faced extinction. They wrote: "[The] real threat to [the recording companies] may be a loss of control, and

vulnerability to replacement by a more internet-friendly distrib-
utor of music in the new economy." [55]

Chris Gorog, the CEO of multimedia software company
Roxio, Inc., criticized the music industry for not doing enough
to take advantage of Internet technology, writing: "The record
companies and movie studios have come to Washington saying,
'the illegal shared file services are destroying our business. We
can't compete with free downloads.' An often-overlooked fact in
this debate is—they haven't even tried." [56] While acknowledging
that the challenge is great, Gorog criticized the recording industry for not developing a product on par for what is available
for free, noting:

> An illegal service like Morpheus is indeed the "celestial jukebox".
> One can access virtually any song in the world, download it
> and burn it to CD. A very attractive proposition. MusicNet,
> on the other hand, the service owned by Warner Bros and
> BMG, doesn't even offer their own complete catalogs . . . and
> what they do offer must stay on your PC. I haven't been to too
> many parties where everybody gathers around the computer
> to listen to tunes. [57]

Gorog also blasted the industry for not using its media
clout for aggressive promotion of the legitimate download
services, noting:

> The five major record labels are each involved in legal music
> download services. These companies are part of the largest
> communications conglomerates in the world and yet, have you
> seen a single advertisement for the services they own; MusicNet
> or Pressplay? They could be promoting their services with
> their movies and television shows, at their retail outlets and
> theme parks, but instead—nothing. A cynic might conclude
> that they have absolutely no intention of making these on-line
> ventures successful. [58]

Attacks on P2P networks threaten the Internet's legitimate uses.

Facing frustration in their lawsuits against the newer file-sharing services such as KaZaA, Morpheus, and Grokster, the recording industry has taken to what it calls "self-help" measures (critics call it vigilantism), saying that the industry is taking the laws into its own hands. Self-help measures basically involve using computer technology, rather than the court system, to make song swapping more difficult. People using file-sharing networks are generally searching for songs by their favorite artists. Some artists have made it more difficult to find their songs by filling P2P networks with "spoof" files, which appear to the user to be the song in question but are really something else, such as a poor recording or static. Software companies, including Overpeer and Media-Defender, help artists and record labels flood P2P networks with spoof files, a process often referred to as "decoying."

A more controversial means of self-help is "interdiction," which some people have likened to a "denial of service" attack, a common weapon of hackers. A denial of service attack, usually driven by a virus secretly spread to thousands of computers, results when thousands of computers try to access a company's website or e-mail system at the same time. The website or e-mail system can only handle a limited number of requests at the same time, and therefore, people who want to visit the website or send e-mail cannot do so because the company's computers are tied up by the unexpected Internet traffic. Interdiction works in a similar way: The program looks for copyrighted files that are available for download and then repeatedly downloads them at very slow speeds. By doing so, the program prevents other users from downloading the song from that particular computer.

The developers of file-sharing software have reacted angrily to tactics such as decoying and interdiction. Steve Griffin, the CEO of StreamCast, which distributes Morpheus software, said that such tactics "are not self-help tools, they are subversive tactics to attack the very person that media companies are trying to market to, the consumer."[59] In an interview with internetnews.com, he likened the use of these and similar techniques to a "declaration of cyber warfare on the consumer."[60]

While file-sharing companies are understandably concerned that the so-called "self-help" measures make their products more difficult to use, other people are concerned that tying up traffic on P2P networks will lead to a general slowdown of the Internet. During a 2002 hearing, Rep. Rick Boucher of Virginia raised a number of questions about the effect of self-help technology on legitimate use of the Internet by others:

> Would any of these intended self-help mechanisms harm innocent Internet users by perhaps slowing down the speed of a shared network, such as a cable modem service? . . . What are the implications for the Internet's functionality when the inevitable arms race develops and countermeasures are used to block self-help mechanisms? I can imagine that if the recording industry launches what amounts to a denial of service attack against Internet users, that denial of service attacks will, in turn, be launched against the industry, with broad, adverse effects on Internet speed to the disadvantage of Internet users generally.[61]

Summary

Many people consider peer-to-peer (P2P) networks to be one of the Internet's most valuable offerings. Artists have benefited from the publicity generated by making their songs available on P2P networks, and consumers have been able to expose themselves to new music and share it with their friends. Supporters of file sharing say that P2P networks have many legitimate uses, and that efforts by the recording industry to destroy them are wrong.

File Sharing Is Online Piracy That Harms Artists

For football players, the road to the Super Bowl is a long and winding one. For Michelle Maalouf, however, the journey was even stranger. Her father had purchased a computer and signed up for a high-speed Internet connection with the local cable company. Like many of their friends, 13-year-old Michelle and her 17-year-old sister began taking advantage of the high-speed connection to download music—a lot of music. Using KaZaA file-sharing software, they were able to download songs by a wide variety of artists from the hard drives of Internet users all over the world. In all, the two had almost 2,000 songs stored on their computer.

The Maalouf sisters, however, were not the only people taking advantage of the family's high-speed connection. Other KaZaA users were able to download music from the Maaloufs' computer. In fact, KaZaA users prefer to download music from people who have high-speed connections, making their computers so-called "supernodes" for file sharing. Unless special steps are taken, people who use KaZaA to copy music from others also open their music files for copying. Security experts warn that a user's hard drive can be open in other less desirable ways, allowing hackers to steal sensitive information and making the system vulnerable to viruses. In fact, the Maalouf family had to erase their hard drive, including the music library, when a virus found its way onto their computer via KaZaA.

The computer virus was the least of the Maaloufs' problems. In August 2003, the girls' father received a notice from the cable company that the Recording Industry Association of America (RIAA) had obtained a court order requiring the company to disclose Raymond Maalouf's identity to the RIAA. The industry group, which represents recording companies, was suing people who had made large numbers of copyrighted songs available on their hard drive. Although the girls said publicly that they did not realize that they were doing anything wrong, the Maaloufs were forced into defending themselves against a lawsuit seeking thousands of dollars for making the songs available in violation of U.S. copyright laws. The songwriters, musicians, and artists who owned the copyrights on the recordings had not sanctioned (given consent for) sharing songs on KaZaA, and the creators of the music made no money from the trading of songs on KaZaA.

The industry group began filing lawsuits against individual computer users as part of a losing battle against unsanctioned file sharing. Although the entertainment industry had succeeded in stopping Napster from providing a central database of songs that could be downloaded without paying the owner of the copyright, other services such as KaZaA and Grokster quickly took over the market. In these new networks, individual computers, such as the Maaloufs' computer, served both as the source of the songs and the list of what was available. The RIAA realized that to stop the file sharing at its source, the group would have to pursue individual users, including the Maaloufs.

Another part of the recording industry's battle against unsanctioned file sharing was a renewed effort to get file swappers to "go legit" by paying for the songs that they downloaded. Apple Computer, for example, launched iTunes Music Store, which offered thousands of songs that could be downloaded—with the songwriters' and artists' permission—for 99 cents each. As part of a massive promotion, Apple partnered with Pepsi to give away 100 million free songs to Pepsi drinkers with winning bottle caps. To kick off the campaign, the companies aired television commercials during the Super Bowl, which sometimes attracts as much attention for its ads as for its on-field action. With "I Fought the Law and the Law Won" playing in the background, Michelle and other teens sued by the RIAA appeared in a commercial urging people to download songs from the Internet—legally, using iTunes.

The RIAA and many other people involved in the entertainment industry take a dim view of peer-to-peer networks, which they view as a threat to their business interests. While peer-to-peer networks do have some legitimate uses, such as sharing the music of artists who consent to copying or sharing such information as recipes or scientific data, these uses represent only a small fraction of the activity on peer-to-peer networks. The vast majority of files that are exchanged contain copyrighted material, distributed without any compensation to the person who created the music. Such exchanges are a form of piracy that deprive songwriters, musicians, and others of the royalties upon which they depend in order to make a living. Although the record industry has been slow to develop technologies for online music sales, the proliferation of peer-to-peer networks offering free copies of copyrighted material has made it very difficult to establish a market for legitimate sales of music online. Because regulating peer-to-peer networks has proven so difficult, the music industry wants the authority to take the law into its own hands, running software that will tie up the computers of people trying to share files and otherwise frustrate the efforts of people seeking illegitimate copies of copyrighted material.

> • **Do you think services that charge money to download songs will be successful?**

An overwhelming amount of P2P use infringes on copyright.

The RIAA and other opponents of unsanctioned file sharing reject comparisons between file-sharing programs and other more established technologies that can also be used to duplicate copyrighted material. The difference between programs such as KaZaA and Grokster on the one hand and photocopiers and VCRs on the other hand, the RIAA maintains, is that photocopiers and VCRs have many legitimate uses. Although a photocopier can be used to make illegal copies of books or sheet music for sale, it can also be used by businesses to make copies of business documents or by teachers to make copies of tests— copying that does not violate anyone's copyright. Although a VCR can be used to make bootleg copies of movies for sale, it can also be used to record shows for viewing in the home, which is a legal "fair use" of copyrighted television programs.

The biggest problem with comparing services such as KaZaA and Grokster to photocopiers and VCRs is that evidence gathered by the recording industry shows that an overwhelming majority of the files traded using such programs contain copyrighted material. Although it is true that peer-to-peer networks can be used to exchange material that is not copyrighted, such material can also be posted on websites, distributed by e-mail, or exchanged by other means. A person has nothing to fear by posting uncopyrighted material on a website, but a peer-to-peer network makes the unauthorized distribution of copyrighted materials more difficult to trace and shut down. Because there is no real need to distribute uncopyrighted material using peer-to-peer networks—as opposed to websites—most of the material exchanged on peer-to-peer networks is copyrighted material. In fact, in a lawsuit against Grokster and MusicCity, a group of music publishers charged that they owned the copyright to 75 percent of the files available through Grokster and that, in total, 90 percent of the files on Grokster likely infringed their copyrights or the copyrights of others.[62]

FROM THE BENCH

Downloading Copyrighted Songs Is Not a "Fair Use"

In shutting down Napster, a federal court rejected the company's argument that the use of its software for sampling (or "try-it-before-you-buy-it") was acceptable under copyright law, whether or not it led to increased CD sales.

The district court determined that sampling remains a commercial use even if some users eventually purchase the music. [F]ree promotional downloads are highly regulated by the record company plaintiffs and that the companies collect royalties for song samples available on retail Internet sites. [The] free downloads provided by the record companies consist of thirty- to sixty-second samples or are full songs programmed to "time out," that is, exist only for a short time on the downloader's computer. In comparison, Napster users download a full, free and permanent copy of the recording.

The record supports the district court's preliminary determinations that: (1) The more music that sampling users download, the less likely they are to eventually purchase the recordings on audio CD; and (2) even if the audio CD market is not harmed, Napster has adverse effects on the developing digital download market.

Napster further argues that the district court erred in rejecting its evidence that the users' downloading of "samples" increases or tends to increase audio CD sales. The district court, however, correctly noted that "any potential enhancement of plaintiffs' sales would not tip the fair use analysis conclusively in favor of defendant." . . . We agree that increased sales of copyrighted material attributable to unauthorized use should not deprive the copyright holder of the right to license the material. Nor does positive impact in one market, here the audio CD market, deprive the copyright holder of the right to develop identified alternative markets, here the digital download market.

Source: *A&M Records, Inc. v. Napster, Inc.,* 239 F.3d 1004 (9th Cir. 2001)

Song swapping harms the creators and distributors of music.

Although the Supreme Court has yet to rule on the issue, lower courts and many lawmakers seem to agree that copying songs on a peer-to-peer network is not a "fair use" of copyrighted material. Some proponents of file sharing have said that song swapping qualifies as a fair use permitted by copyright law because people are not selling the songs and because the songs are for their own personal use. The trial judge in the Napster case rejected this idea, however, finding:

> [G]iven the vast scale of Napster use among anonymous individuals, the court finds that downloading and uploading MP3 music files with the assistance of Napster are not private uses. At the very least, a host user sending a file cannot be said to engage in a personal use when distributing that file to an anonymous requester. Moreover, the fact that Napster users get for free something they would ordinarily have to buy suggests that they reap economic advantages from Napster use.[63]

Testifying before Congress in 2001, country music singer-songwriter Lyle Lovett noted that copyright protection of songs enables songwriters to make a living and that allowing copyright laws to be weakened would discourage people from pursuing careers as songwriters. He said:

> My songs . . . are truly my creations—extensions of who I am and what I believe. But, my songs also are my livelihood. If I can't earn a living from them, I'll have to do something else. And if every songwriter is unable to earn a living from creating music, if every songwriter has to do something else to make ends meet, who will write the songs of America and the world? I love what I do. But this is a tough business. And to illustrate that, I would ask . . . this question: Have you ever seen in the classified section of any newspaper an ad which

reads: "Songwriter wanted. Good salary. Paid vacation. Health benefits and many other perks." I'm sure you haven't. Most songwriters are lonely entrepreneurs trying again and again for that hit which will help them take care of their families and keep them writing in the hopes of another hit down the road so that songwriting can be a career, not a part-time unpaid struggle. In my case, it took many years and many songs before I had that first hit. However, success would be meaningless without strong copyright laws . . . [because] it is only through the protection of the copyright law . . . that our right to earn a living from our creative work is assured.[64]

Answering arguments that artists can benefit from file-sharing networks because of the potential for generating publicity, Lovett said:

I have no objection to songwriters or performers agreeing that their work be free on the Internet or anywhere else if they want. Some have made that choice. But for me, and for the overwhelming majority of my songwriter and performer colleagues, our choice is that we be compensated for the use of our creative work, which is our property.[65]

With the sale of any CD or an authorized download through a service like iTunes Music Store, the performer of the song receives a payment called a "royalty" for each copy sold, and the songwriter also receives a royalty set by federal law at about eight cents per song. When a store sells a Lyle Lovett CD, he receives royalties as both singer and songwriter. Of course, many recording artists perform other people's songs. When a store sells a CD with Vanessa Williams singing "Save the Best for Last," she receives a royalty for the performance, but the song-writer—in this case Phil Galdston—receives a songwriting royalty. When someone swaps a song on the Internet without permission, however, the performer and songwriter receive nothing. Testifying before the same Congressional subcommittee in 2002, Galdston said:

> The . . . angry talk about the major record companies, and their failings (you know, "Why should I pay $18.00 for a CD with only one good song on it?" and the like), when applied to the debate about unauthorized downloading ignores this essential fact of ownership. So, a person who downloads a record without authorization may be trying to punish what they believe are big, bad record companies and greedy, selfish artists. But they're punishing songwriters like me, the people in the creative process who can least afford to be punished. When I license a song to a record company, I receive no fee, no advance, no payment of any kind. I will only receive compensation when, and if, the recording of my song sells.[66]

Galdston also made clear that the supposed benefits that recording labels and performers might gain from allowing song swapping do not help songwriters:

> There are artists, labels, and artist-songwriters who may very well benefit from permitting audience members to download their work for free. Unlike pure songwriters, artists and labels have alternate sources of income and long-range goals to promote. Celine Dion or Brandy or Beyoncé Knowles may profit more from the sales of concert tickets or t-shirts than they lose from a free download promoting their merchandise. The artist and label may decide that it is more profitable to offer a free download in return for, say, an audience member's e-mail address. That trade provides them with an opportunity to market other products and services. Simply put, that is their choice; it should not be imposed on me.[67]

- **Are CDs priced fairly?**

The recording industry cannot compete with pirated material.

Galdston's comments reflect a common excuse given by song swappers to justify their actions—that file sharing only hurts greedy, giant corporations, like recording companies and movie studios that have brought the problem on themselves by not jumping headfirst into Internet technology. A common complaint is that the paid services do not offer "one-stop shopping," because different recording labels have different songs in their catalogs. As Hilary Rosen, chairman and CEO of the RIAA explained at the same hearing, however, legitimate services have to comply with complicated legal requirements that song-swapping services simply ignore. She testified:

> There is no substitute for giving consumers what they want. The record industry, it has been repeated multiple times, was slow to get there. But now there are legitimate services up and available. They clearly don't have as much music as the pirate services, because [unauthorized services] don't have to worry about finding copyright owners to make sure that they get paid and are licensed.[68]

The real problem facing the entertainment industry in competing with file-sharing services is very simple: price. As Rep. Martin Meehan remarked during the House hearing, "When you have two identical products—one that is free that you can download, as millions and millions of Americans apparently are, and then you have another one that has a price tag—obviously, free wins every time."[69] A number of people have argued that if the recording industry set low enough prices for song downloads, people might choose the reliability of legitimate downloads over the hassles of file sharing—having to sort through "spoofed" files and worrying about viruses, for example. At the same hearing, however, Rep. Darrell Issa rejected the "theory that piracy is the result of unreasonable prices by the copyright holders," noting,

"Statements like 'reasonable prices' are in fact not part of the copy-right, patent, or trademark debate." Just as shoplifting overpriced items is wrong, Rep. Issa believes that song swapping is wrong, no matter what the recording industry decides to charge for song downloads. He stated that if recording labels "choose to put their product on at $29.95 or at $.99, that is a business decision that they have to make consistent with the constitutional protection that they were clearly granted by our Founding Fathers."[70]

It seems that the file-sharing industry is always one step ahead of the entertainment industry. When a federal court shut down Napster's free service, new services sprang up that took advantage of the legal technicalities of the Napster ruling. Napster had operated a centralized file server (a computer accessible by Internet) listing the songs that were available on individual users' computers, and the court ruled that operating this file server, thus enabling users to find and trade songs, showed that Napster knew that copyrights were being violated and made Napster responsible for the trading of copyrighted files. New services such as KaZaA, Grokster, and Morpheus did not use the central file server and took further steps to isolate themselves from being a party to the illegal file swapping. For example, the new services encrypted information, meaning that the companies could not identify which files its users were trading. At least one federal court has ruled that by taking these steps, these services had effectively shielded themselves from legal responsibility for copyright infringement taking place on the networks. In a case involving Grokster and Morpheus software, California-based federal judge Stephen Wilson ruled:

> This Court is not blind to the possibility that Defendants may have intentionally structured their businesses to avoid sec-ondary liability for copyright infringement, while benefiting financially from the illicit draw of their wares. . . . To justify a judicial remedy, however, Plaintiffs invite this Court to expand existing copyright law beyond its well-drawn boundaries.[71]

Although other courts are free to disagree with Judge Wilson's decision, the recording industry definitely faces barriers in suing the manufacturers of file-sharing software. As a result of the difficulties, RIAA began to go after individual file swappers, such as teenager Michelle Maalouf and her family. The recording industry found the names and addresses of file swappers by sending subpoenas—legal documents requesting information—to the file swappers' Internet Service Providers (ISPs). The recording industry was relying on a federal law called the Digital Millennium Copyright Act (DMCA), which allows a copyright owner to force ISPs to remove unauthorized material from their servers. Earthlink, America Online, and other ISPs not only provide Internet access to homes, schools, and businesses but also host websites by running file servers. The DMCA made it much easier for a copyright owner to use a subpoena to find out the name and address of someone who posted unauthorized material on a website hosted by the ISP. Essentially, under DMCA, the copyright owner merely needed a signature from a court employee whereas the traditional subpoena process required a court hearing.

The recording industry believed that the DMCA was broad enough to cover peer-to-peer networks and that ISPs would be required to provide information about subscribers sharing copyrighted material on their own computers. The industry began flooding ISPs with subpoenas to find out the identities of song swappers. In December 2003, however, a federal court dealt the recording industry a setback by ruling that the protections offered by the DMCA to copyright owners did not include protections against file sharing by individual users. The court noted the important difference between the act of hosting a website, in which the ISP stores the unauthorized materials on its file servers, and the act of providing Internet connections (through dial-up, DSL, or cable) to people who swap songs stored on their own computers. In *RIAA* v. *Verizon Internet Services,* the court ruled that because an ISP acts as a "mere conduit" when it provides an Internet connection to a song swapper, the DMCA did not apply, and the recording industry could not take advantage of the quick and easy subpoena process to go after song swappers.[72]

As a result of the *Verizon* decision, the recording industry has been forced to resort to so-called "John Doe" lawsuits, because the identity of the people being sued is unknown. The recording industry brings lawsuits against unknown people using specific Internet addresses and then seeks—during the course of the lawsuit—to find out the identities of these people from their ISPs. Obviously, this is much more complicated than simply requesting the information from the ISP through a simple subpoena process. Because the *Verizon* decision was issued by a local court rather than the Supreme Court, other local courts are free to disagree with the ruling. The decision, however, is expected to influence other courts.

"Self-help" technology is needed to fight P2P networks.

The court system operates slowly and has been a continual source of setbacks to the entertainment industry. In the meantime, Internet users continue to download songs, making it less likely that these users will ever purchase authorized copies of those songs and are therefore depriving the entertainment industry and individual songwriters and musicians of income. To stem the losses, the entertainment industry has expressed a desire to use so-called "self-help" methods instead of relying on the court system to stop unauthorized song swapping. Self-help essentially means that copyright owners, such as songwriters or recording companies, can go after song swappers without having to rely on the court system or filing a complaint with authorities.

Opponents of self-help methods have characterized the techniques as vigilantism, but self-help is not really "taking the law into your own hands" if it is allowed by law. Randy Saaf, CEO of MediaDefender, a manufacturer of software that

License to hack

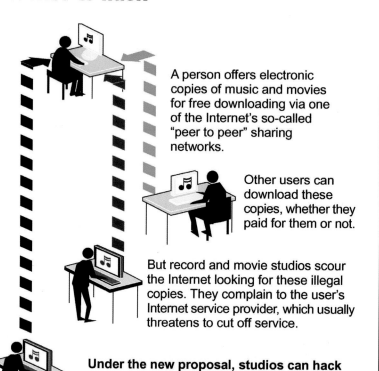

A person offers electronic copies of music and movies for free downloading via one of the Internet's so-called "peer to peer" sharing networks.

Other users can download these copies, whether they paid for them or not.

But record and movie studios scour the Internet looking for these illegal copies. They complain to the user's Internet service provider, which usually threatens to cut off service.

Under the new proposal, studios can hack directly into a person's computer to disable sharing the copyrighted file, or they can knock the computer offline.

SOURCE: Associated Press   AP

Until the courts pass legislation banning peer-to-peer (P2P) services like KaZaA from allowing their users to swap copyrighted files, the recording industry has instituted "self-help" technological measures to address the problem. Current techniques include uploading thousands of "decoy" files onto the network to make copyrighted files more difficult to find. The industry would also like to be able to hack into a user's computer or knock the computer offline to prevent the user from sharing the copyrighted files.

copyright owners can use to disrupt P2P networks explained that some of the techniques were well within the law. For example, decoying involves putting thousands of fake files on the networks, making it more difficult for users to find copyrighted material. Calling decoying "clearly lawful," Saaf noted that MediaDefender simply placed files in the P2P network, just as any other user would:

> Decoying is accomplished by passively acting as a member of the P2P network on the Internet public space and allowing thousands of files to be downloaded from our computers. The primary purpose of Decoying is to create a needle in a haystack situation that makes the pirated content difficult to find. All P2P networks have two basic functionalities: search and file transfer. Decoying only affects the search functionality of a P2P network and does nothing to the file transfer side. The pirated material is still there on the network, but it is harder to find.[73]

Saaf, however, testified that anti-hacking laws, which were originally designed to protect the security of data, could be interpreted to outlaw another technique called interdiction. He urged Congress to support a measure proposed by Rep. Howard Berman of California, which would legalize self-help techniques—such as interdiction—that involved connecting to a user's computer. He testified that the technique should not be considered a form of hacking because it did not threaten the user's data or operating system in any way, noting:

> I want to make it clear that MediaDefender agrees that any anti-piracy solution on a P2P network has to be non-invasive. Peoples' computers and files should never be harmed under any circumstance. However, any P2P anti-piracy technology will inevitably involve communication with individuals' computers located on the P2P network. . . . Interdiction only

targets uploaders of pirated material. The way it targets them is to simply download the pirated file. MediaDefender's computers hook up to the person using the P2P protocol being targeted and download the pirated file at a throttled down speed. . . . Interdiction works by getting in front of potential downloaders when someone is serving pirated content using a P2P network. When MediaDefender's computer's see someone making a copyrighted file available for upload, our computers simply hook into that computer and download the file. The goal is not to absorb all of that user's bandwidth but block connections to potential downloaders. . . . The beauty of Interdiction is that it does not affect anything on that computer except the ability to upload pirated files on that particular P2P network. The computer user still has full access to e-mail, web, and other file sharing programs. Interdiction does not even affect a user's ability to download files, even pirated files, on the P2P network while their computer is being Interdicted. . . . Legislation like Congressman Berman's peer-to-peer bill helps clarify that non-invasive self-help technologies, such as Interdiction, are a legitimate form of copyright protection.[73]

> • **Should record companies get to break the law in order to stop illegal song swapping?**

Although file-sharing advocates have criticized interdiction and similar techniques as invading computer users' privacy, Rep. Berman believes that such complaints are hypocritical because the file-sharing software itself is an even greater threat to security than self-help measures are:

If piracy profiteers were truly concerned about security and privacy threats to P2P users, they would address the security and privacy threats posed by the P2P networks themselves. . . . Gnutella, and other popular P2P networks expose P2P users to spyware, trojan horses, system exploits, denial of service attacks, worms, and viruses[, and] . . . the vast majority of P2P users are exposing personal information, such as credit card numbers, to every other P2P user. . . . Do the piracy profiteers talk about these real security and privacy concerns? No. And you know why? Because it is the piracy profiteers who put the spyware on the computers of P2P users so they can surreptitiously collect their personal information and sell it to third parties.[75]

Summary

Most recording companies, songwriters, and musicians object to having their work distributed for free through file-sharing networks like KaZaA, Morpheus, and Grokster. Free, unauthorized song swapping makes it impossible for the music industry to compete and therefore deprives musicians and songwriters of income for their work. The recording industry believes that it needs greater power to use technology to disrupt the sharing of copyrighted material on peer-to-peer networks.

The Government Should Not Try to Regulate E-mail

I n the 1930s, meatpacking giant Hormel offered the public the opportunity to win $100 for naming its new product, a canned spiced ham. The winner was the simple but catchy "Spam." In the 1970s, British comedy troupe Monty Python poked fun at Spam in an absurd sequence in which a cafe offers menu items including "spam, bacon, sausage and spam" and "spam, egg, spam, spam, bacon and spam."[76] Inexplicably, the cafe is filled with Vikings who repeatedly sing "Spam, spam, spam, spam" over and over. By the end of the skit, viewers are pretty tired of hearing the word "spam." As Internet users began to notice an increasing number of e-mail messages offering products and services for sale, "spam" seemed to be an appropriate nickname for the repeated annoying messages.

Spam annoys people for many reasons. Some people just do not like to be bothered by sales pitches. Other people are offended by pornographic spam, which is fairly common. Too many spam messages offer fraudulent promises like "get-rich-quick" schemes. From a business standpoint, ISPs do not like having to devote bandwidth and server space to transmitting and storing spam. Internet users, however, are not powerless to defend themselves against spam. Many commonsense steps can be taken to reduce spam, most notably using spam filters. In much the same way that filtering software blocks porno-graphic websites, e-mail filters block spam from reaching a user's in-box.

With technological solutions available, many believe that the government should not be in the business of trying to regulate e-mail to prevent spam. Government regulation has a difficult time keeping up with technology generally, and any restrictions on a means of communication raise possibilities of infringement upon free speech. In 2003, Congress passed the Controlling the Assault of Non-Solicited Pornography and Marketing Act, or CAN-SPAM Act. Although not an outright prohibition on spamming, the law does place some restrictions upon e-mail marketers. Many people are calling on Congress to pass stronger legislation, but others question whether any laws are necessary. Critics say anti-spam laws are unnecessary, ineffective, and unconstitutional, and that Internet users and ISPs should be left to develop their own solutions to unwanted e-mail.

- **Do you get spam? How much inconvenience does it cause you?**

The spam problem is greatly exaggerated.

Many people believe that the anti-spam backlash is making a mountain out of a molehill. Although many people might find spam somewhat annoying, it is undeniable that e-mail is also a great way to advertise. It is quick, cheap, and unlike junk mail, does not result in trees being cut down. Some people actually like receiving so-called "Spam," because it helps them find good deals on products that they would buy anyway. Most importantly, advertising by e-mail is a lot less intrusive than other forms of sales pitches. By simply hitting the delete button, an uninterested buyer can make spam disappear, which is a lot easier than having to answer a telemarketing call during supper or trying to get rid of a door-to-door salesperson.

Ronald Scelson has built his Louisiana-based company from the ground up into a successful business by sending approximately 180 million e-mails per day. He flatly rejects the idea that spam is nothing but a nuisance. While acknowledging that a small minority of people complain loudly about spam, he testified before a Senate committee that many people do not object to spam. The proof, he said, was that his e-mail marketing campaigns continued to be successful. He noted:

> The reason e-mail has grown is people still buy. My average complaint ratio is 1,000 people [out of 180 million] complain, close to 2,000 remove in a mailing and a 1 to 2 percent response rate. If it's hated so bad, which people do complain, then why do more people buy than they complain about it?[77]

One to two percent of 180 million e-mails daily translates into a lot of sales, but Scelson complains that his Louisiana-based company is burdened with regulations not affecting other advertisers. The man labeled by critics as the "Cajun Spammer" complained to the Senate committee that regulating e-mail solicitation more heavily than bulk postal mail made little sense from the standpoint of protecting either individual privacy or the environment:

> The differences between [bulk e-mail and bulk postal mail] are that when you receive mail at your home, you open it, read it if you want, then throw it in the trash. You then have to carry that trash to the curb, where it is then hauled away and used as landfill (like we don't have enough trash already).

Not to mention the trees that are cut down for the paper used! Then there is the Electronic Mail (E-Mail). If you don't want it, just check off DELETE. No mess, no cleanup, no pollution. I think my way is better![78]

Rebuffing claims that spam imposes great costs on Internet service providers by using so much bandwidth, Scelson says that ISPs brought the costs upon themselves by adopting e-mail filters. In addition to spending heavily on expensive filtering technology, the filtering technology has led spammers to send e-mail in a way that uses even more bandwidth. Because e-mail filters block e-mails sent to large numbers of people, spammers must send individual e-mails to each recipient. This uses more bandwidth than the prior practice of sending a single e-mail to hundreds of recipients. As Scelson explained:

> Part of ISPs Anti-spam filters do not allow high "BCC" (blind carbon copy) I could set my BCC setting to 500 for every 500 people who get this email I will use up a total of 33k in size (est. the ad is 33k). Since this filter is in place, I have to mail at 1 BCC, which means that if I send an ad to 500 people then it would be like 500 times 33k. Now I have consumed 1.6 megabytes of bandwidth for those 500 people. So, now you see why their cost went up.[79]

The CAN-SPAM Act and other Anti-spam laws will not work.

Many people believe that members of Congress were grandstanding when they passed the CAN-SPAM Act. They accuse politicians of trying to make it seem like they were doing something about a very unpopular issue. In addition to saying that the so-called "spam problem" has been blown out of proportion, these critics say that the CAN-SPAM Act is not even a solution because it will not work. Critics of the CAN-SPAM Act have derisively called it the "You Can Spam Act" because it does not really prohibit spam. For most commercial messages, the sender must offer the recipient the opportunity to "opt out" of future mailings. While subsequent mailings would be prohibited by the law, the law does nothing to stop the initial message. Taking into account the countless thousands of marketers, those initial e-mails will still mean that a lot of messages will be allowed. Many people have said that by allowing marketers "one bite at

THE LETTER OF THE LAW

The CAN-SPAM Act

Whoever, in or affecting interstate or foreign commerce, knowingly:

(1) accesses a protected computer without authorization, and intentionally initiates the transmission of multiple commercial electronic mail messages from or through such computer,

(2) uses a protected computer to relay or retransmit multiple commercial electronic mail messages, with the intent to deceive or mislead recipients, or any Internet access service, as to the origin of such messages,

(3) materially falsifies header information in multiple commercial electronic mail messages and intentionally initiates the transmission of such messages,

(4) registers, using information that materially falsifies the identity of the actual registrant, for five or more electronic mail accounts or online user accounts or two or more domain names, and intentionally initiates the transmission of multiple commercial electronic mail messages from any combination of such accounts or domain names, or

(5) falsely represents oneself to be the registrant or the legitimate successor in interest to the registrant of 5 or more Internet Protocol addresses, and intentionally initiates the transmission of multiple commercial electronic mail messages from such addresses, or conspires to do so, shall be punished [by a fine or imprisonment of up to five years, or both].

Source: 18 U.S.C. § 1037.

the apple," the CAN-SPAM Act actually legalizes the type of spam that some states have sought to ban.

Although the law imposes stricter requirements on sexually oriented e-mails, many people doubt that spam laws, even strict ones, will work. First, many people believe that spammers will ignore the CAN-SPAM Act, just as they have ignored state anti-spam laws. As Ronald Scelson noted, the temptation to make money will probably lead many spammers to avoid the law's requirements:

> If we use ADV . . . we are blocked. If we use Remove or unsub-scribe, we are blocked. If we use [a] "From" address that is valid, we are blocked. If we send too many emails from one IP, we are blocked. So, we have two options . . . Break the law and stay in business or do it legal and go out of business.[80]

Perhaps one reason that spammers are so willing to ignore the laws is that they have generally been tricky enough to avoid detection. Although the CAN-SPAM Act bans disguising the source of e-mail, this very tactic can make tracking down a spammer very difficult. Even when spammers are caught, collecting money from them, either as fines or as judgments in private lawsuits brought by ISPs, can be difficult. Because most spammers are not legitimate, well-established busi-nesses, they are unlikely to have enough money to pay fines or lawsuits.

E-mail easily can be sent across international borders, and enforcing anti-spam laws internationally will be very difficult, writes law professor Anita Ramasastry. In a column for *Findlaw's Writ*, she writes that a great deal of spam already originates over-seas, citing a flood of financial scams from Nigeria. Typically, recipients were asked to send a small amount of "up-front" money to help a Nigerian citizen transfer a large amount of money out of the country. Of course, the victims of the scam never saw the reward that they had been promised, and authorities could do nothing to help them recover the money that they had lost. Ramasastry notes, "It will be difficult to find international spammers and to bring them to justice—even when we do know who they are, which is rare."[81]

Another effect of anti-spam laws, Ramasastry predicts, is that many U.S.-based spammers will move their operations overseas—as Internet gambling, pornography, and file-sharing companies have done—to escape U.S. law enforcement. Scelson pointed out the downside of this exodus to the Senate: "You passed the laws. We go outside the U.S. Corporations get moved outside the U.S. and from what attorneys have told me, if the corporation, the incoming money and everything is outside the U.S., there's no tax dollars owed in the U.S."[82]

> • In 2003, the House Subcommittee on Crime, Terrorism, and Homeland Security was debating anti-spam laws. Are there more pressing issues?

Broader anti-spam laws would threaten legitimate businesses.

The many people who think that the CAN-SPAM Act is a weak and ineffective law are not necessarily convinced that a stronger law is the right answer. Although it is questionable that the law's focus on fraudulent and pornographic e-mail will minimize the amount of spam accumulating in people's in-boxes, the law's focus on reducing fraud and pornography is partly a result of the business community's strong opposition to banning the practice of advertising by e-mail. In fact, the business community supported the CAN-SPAM Act because businesses wanted to protect the viability of e-mail as a marketing tool. The waves of fraudulent and pornographic e-mail messages threatened to drown out legitimate offers from established businesses, such as Amazon.com.

Many businesses also supported the federal CAN-SPAM Act because designing an advertising campaign to comply with one federal law is much simpler than designing a campaign to comply with dozens of state laws, each with different requirements. Prior to the passage of the federal law, which effectively wiped most of the states' requirements off the books, states had enacted various requirements that businesses found burdensome. For example, some states had required that all e-mails advertising a product or service include "ADV" (for "advertisement") in the subject line of the e-mail. Businesses had opposed such laws because most ISPs would block the messages, and many people would use filtering programs that automatically deleted e-mails labeled as advertisements. As a result, explained Joseph Rubin of the U.S. Chamber of Congress, legitimate businesses suffered. Testifying before a Congressional committee in support of a provision in the CAN-SPAM Act that forbids mandatory labeling, he said:

> The rationale behind this restriction [on mandatory "ADV" labeling] is simple: legitimate companies will comply with regulations, even if they are burdensome and ineffective, but spammers will continue to ignore any and all regulations that they see as restricting their ability to mislead consumers. The goal of legislation should not be to give spammers and criminals a competitive advantage over legitimate companies, but should seek to reign in the fraudulent and misleading activities of spammers.[83]

Online retailer Amazon.com does not send unsolicited e-mails; it only communicates by e-mail with established customers who have indicated an interest in receiving promotional updates. Paul Misener, a vice-president of the company, testified that stiff penalties for honest mistakes would penalize legitimate businesses. He feared that people would be more likely to sue established companies such as Amazon.com than they would be to sue the fraudulent and pornographic spammers whose activities were much more objectionable.

Larger companies, like Amazon.com, are easier to identify than rogue spammers who conceal their identities. Additionally, larger companies are more likely to be able to pay a court's damage award. Misener testified that anti-spam laws should focus on the "true villains," saying:

> Because commercial e-mail necessarily involves computers and human programmers, there have been and will continue to be occasional email mistakes, no matter how many preventative measures are taken. Such truly honest mistakes are rare and certainly are not the cause of the in-box clutter and associated consumer angst that have led us all to this point. Not only are these mistakes expected and essentially not preventable, the harm to consumers is minimal, and there already are strong market forces at work: Reputable companies simply do not want to irritate consumers who have asked not to be bothered. . . . Proscribing such mistakes would have the perverse effect of discouraging email use by the most reputable—and thereby most exposed—companies. Every day, Amazon.com sends tens of thousands of emails to our customers and, thus, just one simple mistake (such as accidentally sending a notice of a new jazz CD release to customers who have elected not to receive email on jazz music) could expose us to astronomical penalties. Surely, this is not the goal of anti-spam legislation.[84]

The spam problem is best resolved by the free market.

Many people say that relying on the government for protection from spam is not a very wise course of action, especially because Internet users have many ways to reduce the amount of spam they receive. Common techniques for reducing spam are very basic and include using widely available filtering software; not posting e-mail addresses online, where "harvesting" programs can add them to mailing lists; not providing e-mail addresses when filling out forms; and setting up a free "junk" account that can be discontinued. Most of all, experts recommend, never respond to spam, whether to buy or to "unsubscribe," because a response will only lead to more spam. As Ramasastry puts it, "[S]elf-help may still be the best remedy for the headache caused by spam."[85]

The Cato Institute, a Washington, D.C.-based libertarian organization that generally opposes excessive government regulations of all types, believes that the spam problem will eventually take care of itself without government interference. The organization's Wayne Crews points to the use of filtering software as one of many steps that Internet users can take to protect themselves against spam.

> The basic instructions to Internet users still apply: Read the fine print before filling out forms; don't post your email address on Usenet posting or in chat rooms . . . [and] try to avoid posting your email on your website. If need be, set up a separate "junk" email account to use in online interactions. Finally, don't respond to spam, even to ask to be removed since this is often just a trick to assure that an email address is live. Instead, report and send the spam, either to your ISP (which reports it to the spammer's ISP and which might help since most ISPs have "no spam" stipulations as part of their terms of service) or to a service like SpamCop.[86]

Additionally, Crews told a Congressional committee, the Internet industry and software companies are better positioned than the federal government is to combat the proliferation of spam, because they continue to develop new solutions. Unlike legislation, which would allow punishing spammers after the fact, Crews said future technologies could actually prevent spam. One such technology is password-protected e-mail. If someone tries to send an Internet user an e-mail, the user's e-mail program sends back an automated response containing a password. The person sending the e-mail must type in the password for the mail to get through. This effectively blocks spam because spam is generated by computers, and nobody is there to type in the password.

Another technology Crews praised is the idea of charging "postage" for accepting e-mails. Using a technology similar to those used for selling merchandise online, an e-mail user could demand a fee for allowing e-mail to pass. Whereas a fee of a few cents would not deter friends, it might deter spammers. Although Microsoft's Bill Gates supports anti-spam legislation, he has recently embraced the notion of charging postage for receiving e-mail. His proposal had a slight twist: the cost imposed by the sender would not be a financial one but rather a requirement that the computer sending the e-mail perform a complicated calculation that would take several seconds. Although this would not impose a burden on someone sending a few e-mails, performing the calculations would make sending thousands of spam messages an extremely time-consuming process and probably force spammers to purchase many additional computers.

> • **Do you think that e-mail spam filters work?**

Anti-spam laws are unconstitutional.

Regardless of whether or not spam is annoying, most spam is protected by the First Amendment, which prohibits the government from restricting freedom of speech. In fact, it is annoying speech that is probably most needful of First Amendment protection because universally popular speech does not need protection. An exception is that spam that meets the legal definition of "obscenity" is not protected by the First Amendment, although a great deal of "R-rated" and even "XXX-rated" material is covered by the First Amendment. (The law in the area is so confusing that the line between acceptable and obscene is anybody's guess.) Additionally, fraudulent e-mails are not protected by the First Amendment. Even speech that is protected by the First Amendment is subject to some forms of regulation though it cannot be fully suppressed. For spam that is protected by the First Amendment, then, the question for the courts will be whether the regulations burden speech unnecessarily.

Many people believe that the CAN-SPAM Act and other anti-spam laws go too far in regulating lawful speech and are therefore unconstitutional. Law professor Anita Ramasastry believes that the CAN-SPAM Act's focus on e-mails containing advertising runs afoul of previous Supreme Court decisions holding that commercial speech such as advertising is protected by the First Amendment. Although the framers of the Constitution might have enacted the First Amendment primarily to protect criticisms of the government, punishable under British rule, the Supreme Court has made clear that the First Amendment applies to many kinds of speech, and many people believe that it even applies to spam. Ramasastry writes, "[The CAN-SPAM Act] restricts commercial speech. (Indeed, it singles out unsolicited commercial emails—rather than unsolicited charitable or political email, which may be equally unwanted and annoying to some.)"[87] Ramasastry's comments refer to a national "do not spam" registry, which would allow people to shield themselves from commercial spam. Gay-rights groups and anti-abortion groups, however, would still be able to send messages to unwilling recipients.

The problem with the "do not spam" registry, in Ramasastry's view, is that it singles out a legal form of speech for unequal treatment under the law. Another provision of the law that has raised questions among civil libertarians is the requirement that all sexually oriented e-mail be labeled. This not only involves government regulation of a specific form of speech but also sets the table for ISPs to block all e-mails with the label, whether or not individual subscribers want to receive the mail.

The Center for Democracy and Technology, a Washington, D.C.-based organization concerned with the impact of modern technology on civil liberties, has expressed its doubts that spammers will comply with the CAN-SPAM Act's requirement that sexually oriented material be clearly labeled. In comments to the Federal Trade Commission, the federal agency that enforces the CAN-SPAM Act, however, the group noted: "[To] the extent that the labeling requirement is effective, it will be effective in an unconstitutional way, for the label, as used by service providers, will prevent senders of lawful material from reaching willing recipients. . . . [B]ecause the label is intended to interface with ISP filters, the rule would burden senders of lawful, sexually oriented material."[88]

The group pointed out that while some sexually oriented material is considered obscene and is therefore not protected by the First Amendment, a great deal of sexually oriented material is not considered obscene and is therefore protected. The group noted:

> [S]enders of lawful content that discusses, for example, issues related to sexuality or sexual health, will be placed in the difficult position of guessing whether their content must be labeled. Recipients of that legitimate material will be burdened because the filtering technologies that the labeling provision is specifically intended to facilitate will prevent it from reaching their email boxes.[89]

Some civil libertarians have even gone so far as to criticize the CAN-SPAM Act's ban on disguising the source of e-mails. During a 2001 hearing on anti-spam legislation, Wayne Crews of the libertarian Cato Institute said that laws requiring senders of e-mail to identify themselves were a threat to privacy:

> [L]egislative bans on false return e-mail addresses as well as software capable of hiding such information have significant

implications for free speech. Anonymous speech is a corner-stone of our republic. It just happens to be the case that the very technologies that facilitate spam can also protect individuals' identity. As strange as it may sound, spam and the use of spam-ware are means by which individuals create the anonymous leaflet of today.[90]

Summary

Although most people acknowledge that spam can be annoying, many people are convinced that anti-spam laws are not the answer. Citing the possibility of harming legitimate businesses and chilling free speech, critics say that the solution of the so-called "spam problem" is best left to individual Internet users.

Government Regulations Are Needed to Stop Spam

J eannie Wright was fed up with unwanted e-mail messages. Though she never visited pornographic websites, she continually received messages at work prompting her to do so. Some of the 30 pornographic advertisements she received each week even contained explicit photos that she found offensive, and her e-mail program automatically displayed the photos.

One day something happened that prompted the Wyoming woman to write to her congresswoman. U.S. Representative Barbara Cubin read her constituent's letter during a committee hearing about the problems associated with spam. It read: "[L]ast week, my daughter and a client were in my office when a photo of a sexual act appeared on my screen as I was searching for a work-related message I had been expecting. How very embarrassing for me and the client and what a lot to try to explain to my 8-year-old daughter, not to mention my boss."[91]

The sentiments that Ms. Wright expressed in her letter are shared by many Internet users who are increasingly frustrated with the number of unwanted messages appearing in their in-boxes. She wrote:

> These messages make me feel like a victim. Nasty people I do not know and to which I cannot respond are sending me sexually explicit garbage at the place of my work. Many of the messages offer you a link to unsubscribe. Only about 5 percent of those links are legitimate. The rest do not exist. When I try responding to the e-mail messages, those addresses cannot be found, and the e-mail comes back to me. There is no identifying information on these messages, so I can't even call a phone number and demand that it be stopped.[92]

Ms. Wright's complaints did not go completely unheeded as Congress passed the CAN-SPAM Act of 2003. Many have criticized the law as not doing enough to stop the proliferation of spam. Although the law limits fraudulent messages—such as "quick weight loss" plans, herbal sexual potency formulas, and pornographic sales pitches—many people believe that so-called "legitimate" sales pitches by the local tire store are equally annoying because it takes just as much time to delete those messages. Despite the passage of the CAN-SPAM Act and the availability of filtering programs that block spam, many consumer advocates believe that stronger steps are needed. Some have even called for an "opt-in" system, in which an advertiser would need permission before sending an e-mail to an Internet user.

The proliferation of spam threatens the Internet's usefulness.

Although e-mail had been around for years, its popularity exploded in the 1990s. E-mail provided a great way to communicate with friends, family, and anonymous pen-pals around the world. It was quick, and best of all, it was cheap—for the price of an Internet connection, which for many students was free, someone could send an unlimited number of e-mails. Businesses soon found out how useful e-mail could be; it replaced expensive methods of communication such as faxes and Federal Express, and allowed senders to get a message to someone quickly without interrupting the person's day, as a phone call would.

Many of the same advantages led to the proliferation of spam. E-mail users soon found their in-boxes transformed. Once containing only a handful of messages from friends and colleagues, in-boxes began to fill with messages from people trying to sell something. Sometimes, the messages offered a good deal, but too often, they offered deals that were too good to be true. Fraudulent schemes and products such as crash diets, herbal remedies, investment scams, and work-at-home "opportunities" became commonplace. To the dismay of many, advertisements for pornography also began to appear with increasing frequency. To the alarm of parents, many of these advertisements offered a preview of their wares. As the number of spam messages increased, people began to grow frustrated with spam. Polls showed that spam was one of the biggest complaints that most people had with the Internet. Anti-spam groups formed, creating "blacklists" of spammers and urging ISPs to block their e-mails. ISPs began adopting filtering software to prevent users from receiving spam, and many called for Congress to act. Although Congress did not pass an anti-spam law until 2003, more than half the states had responded to widespread complaints by passing anti-spam laws.

Although opponents of anti-spam legislation say that spam is a minimal inconvenience because it can simply be deleted, the sheer volume of spam means that a lot of deleting has to be done. Because so many people receive e-mail on computers they use for work, all of that deleting translates into lost productivity. Citing industry statistics, an attorney for Microsoft told Congress that it costs only about $250 to send a million spam messages, but if the time that it takes to delete all of those messages is measured, it costs about $2,800 in wages—even at minimum wage.[93]

• Has spam made you less interested in using e-mail?

In addition to the inconvenience, supporters of anti-spam legislation have identified three major problems associated with spam: pornography, fraud, and wasted bandwidth and data storage. Bandwidth, or the ability to transmit data, is a major expense for Internet service providers, because as the amount of data transmitted over the Internet increases, ISPs must invest in additional telephone, cable, and fiber optic lines to transmit the data. As more e-mails are transmitted, ISPs must invest in additional computers to store the e-mail. Of course, the higher costs borne by ISPs as a result of spam are ultimately passed on to the consumer in the form of higher monthly access fees. Charles Garry Betty, the chief executive officer of Earthlink, one of the nation's largest ISPs, noted the toll that spam takes on ISPs:

> As an ISP, approximately 50% of all e-mail coming into our servers is spam. AOL estimates this figure as high as 80% on their network. We are able to filter out 70-80% of these messages before they ever get to our customers, but the increasing volume means that lots of unwanted electronic junk mail still gets to user's in-boxes. Spam costs Internet providers real money. Excess server capacity, an "abuse team" working full time to ferret out and close down sources of spam on the internet, internal and external legal fees are all costs we incur because of spam. While we don't publish exact figures on this, it is fair to say that they are in excess of $10 million a year for Earthlink alone.

Spam is a pernicious problem. Whereas get rich quick schemes, effortless weight loss programs and pills that promise to enlarge body parts are nothing new, the cost burden imposed by spam is. Newspaper and magazines ads, telemarketing calls, direct mail pieces, and signs tacked to telephone poles all require the sender to pay for their messages. Spam adds insult to injury by shifting this cost burden. Spam costs virtually nothing to send. (One recent widely circulated spam message for spammers advertises 20 million email addresses for $149). Instead, the costs of spam are borne by ISPs that must handle this junk e-mail and by consumers whose in-boxes are filled with it.[94]

Technological solutions, such as spam filters, are inadequate.

Opponents of anti-spam laws have labeled them unnecessary because of the availability of e-mail filtering programs like Earthlink's spamBlocker. Supporters of such legislation, however, believe that technological measures are only part of the solution. America Online, the nation's largest ISP, filtered as many as 2.4 billion pieces of spam per day in 2003, or about 70 million pieces of spam per day for each AOL subscriber. Despite AOL's efforts, subscribers still received a great deal of spam because spammers are constantly devising new ways to avoid the filtering programs. As Charles Curran, an attorney for AOL put it, "A technical struggle is now taking place on the spam front, one which pits consumers and ISPs using defensive spam filtering technologies against spammers who seek to exploit any technical loophole that will allow them to get their mail through to a recipient's e-mail box."[95]

• **Should ISPs be allowed to block other businesses spam but send subscribers advertisements for the ISPs' own services?**

Legitimate businesses complain that spam filters interfere with the ability of legitimate businesses to communicate with

Canning spam: how to play, and win, the game of e-onslaught

While no one method of defense against unsolicited e-mail is flawless, a combination of weapons used at different levels of transmission can go a long way in stemming the flow.

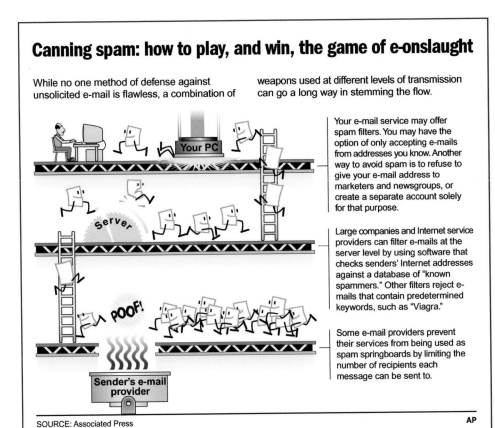

Your e-mail service may offer spam filters. You may have the option of only accepting e-mails from addresses you know. Another way to avoid spam is to refuse to give your e-mail address to marketers and newsgroups, or create a separate account solely for that purpose.

Large companies and Internet service providers can filter e-mails at the server level by using software that checks senders' Internet addresses against a database of "known spammers." Other filters reject e-mails that contain predetermined keywords, such as "Viagra."

Some e-mail providers prevent their services from being used as spam springboards by limiting the number of recipients each message can be sent to.

SOURCE: Associated Press   AP

Despite efforts on the part of the U.S. government to stop the onslaught of spam, or unsolicited e-mails from commercial sources, these messages continue to flood online in-boxes. Both e-mail subscribers and services have responded to the problem by installing e-mail filters on accounts and creating separate e-mail addresses for "junk" e-mail.

their customers. Testifying before the House of Representatives, Joseph Rubin of the U.S. Chamber of Commerce noted that spam filters cannot differentiate between fraudulent and porno-graphic offers on the one hand, and legitimate business pitches on the other. As a result, he said, the legitimate messages of the Chamber's member businesses often fail to reach their intended recipients:

> Retailers, marketers, financial services companies, travel providers, and other businesses that communicate with their customers via e-mail also face serious challenges and expenses as a result of spam. For example, companies must ensure that their communications actually get to their customers, and then need to make sure that their legitimate communications are not deleted along with the spam and pornography that clog their users' e-mail boxes.[96]

Trevor Hughes, executive director of the Network Advertising Initiative, an industry group, expressed his concern to another Congressional committee that e-mail filters even block messages that customers have requested. Examples of so-called "permission-based e-mail" include weekly airline updates on special airfares or updates about a company's newest products. Hughes's organization has formed the E-mail Service Provider Coalition to represent the interests of legitimate businesses that communicate by e-mail without making fraudulent offers or concealing their identity. Hughes called for legislation that would allow ISPs to filter their subscribers' e-mail less aggressively and allow legitimate messages to pass through:

> While spam clearly represents a serious threat to the continued viability of e-mail, the problems created by some of the current tools used to combat spam are equally threatening. Internet Service Providers (ISPs) are aggressively building filtering technologies to limit the amount of spam entering their systems. Conceptually, this is a positive development. However, the spam filters currently in place are creating a new problem: wanted e-mail is not being received. According to a report by Assurance Systems, in the 4th quarter of 2002, an

average of 15% of permission-based email was not received by subscribers to the major ISPs. Some ISPs had non-delivery rates that were startling: NetZero (27%), Yahoo[!] (22%), AOL (18%).[97]

In fact, many filtering programs actually block messages that are not even sales pitches. Many filtering programs employed by ISPs block entire ranges of e-mail addresses because anti-spam groups have put them on their blacklists. For example, people who use a particular e-mail provider or even people in a foreign nation could have their e-mails blocked by the filter because an anti-spam group has identified a large number of spam messages from that e-mail provider or foreign nation. Because filtering programs sometimes block an entire range of addresses, even personal e-mails sometimes are blocked. Chris Murray of Consumers Union complained that even though his e-mail filter had not succeeded in blocking all unwanted spam, it had blocked some important personal messages. He told the House Committee:

> The problem is that filtering technologies are both overbroad and underbroad at the same time. For instance, I [tried] to set up filters on my e-mail system at work. And the problem was that it was filtering some spam, but it was also filtering my colleagues' messages I found out a month later, when they were very angry at me for not showing up at meetings and the like.[98]

The CAN-SPAM Act is a good first step, but stronger laws are needed.

While Congress was deliberating the CAN-SPAM Act, many consumer groups expressed their opinions about what was needed to stop spam. They made numerous suggestions, but some consumer advocates believe Congress was too generous to marketers in the CAN-SPAM Act's final language. Scott Hazen, of the Coalition Against Unsolicited Commercial Email (CAUCE) stated:

> This law does not stop a single spam from being sent. It only makes that spam slightly more truthful. It also gives a federal stamp of approval for every legitimate marketer in the U.S. to start using unsolicited e-mail as a marketing tool. Congress has listened to the marketers and not to consumers, and we have no faith that this law will significantly reduce the amount of spam that American Internet users receive.[99]

CAUCE and other groups are continuing to press for stronger laws, which they believe are needed to curb the flow of spam, rather than the current legislation simply banning fraudulent messages and requiring spammers to include "remove me" links. Among the provisions supported by CAUCE and other groups are requirements that all advertisements be labeled as such in the subject line of the e-mail and that spammers would need advance permission to send advertisements. Additionally, many consumer advocates support allowing Internet users to sue spammers.

After passage of the CAN-SPAM Act, many people expressed disappointment that the law did not ban spamming outright, but instead allowed marketers to send non-fraudulent messages, as long as recipients were given the opportunity to "opt out" of future messages. The problems, consumer advocates say, is that experts recommend never responding to spam—even to opt out—because doing so verifies that the recipient's e-mail address is a valid one, encouraging spammers to send even more spam. Many consumer advocates prefer an "opt-in" law, which would allow businesses to send e-mail only to people who have requested it. Law professor Marc Rotenberg, director of the Electronic Information Privacy Center (EPIC), testified before a Senate committee in support of "a full opt-in regime for unsolicited commercial e-mail except in those cases where a prior business relationship exists." He explained:

> Opt-in is the logical basis for Internet mailings. In fact, most Internet lists today are based on opt-in. These lists typically also provide users with the opportunity to update their contact information and remove themselves from

THE LETTER OF THE LAW

California Tries to Ban Spam

In 2003, the California legislature adopted an "opt-in" system for e-mail, banning all commercial messages not requested by the recipient. The law, however, was effectively wiped off the books by the passage of the weaker CAN-SPAM Act by the U.S. Congress.

Notwithstanding any other provision of law, a person or entity may not do any of the following: (a) Initiate or advertise in an unsolicited commercial e-mail advertisement from California or advertise in an unsolicited commercial e-mail advertisement sent from California. (b) Initiate or advertise in an unsolicited commercial e-mail advertisement to a California electronic mail address, or advertise in an unsolicited commercial e-mail advertisement sent to a California electronic mail address.

"Unsolicited electronic mail advertisement" means any electronic mail advertisement that meets both of the following requirements:

(A) It is addressed to a recipient with whom the initiator does not have an existing business or personal relationship.

(B) It is not sent at the request of or with the express consent of the recipient.

Source: California S.B. 186 (2003)

the list if they choose. There are many opportunities for companies to obtain consent and to build online marketing techniques, in parallel with the traditional Internet lists, which would be welcome by consumers. Where there is a genuine preexisting relationship, then it would be appropriate to communicate by e-mail. Simply visiting a website is not sufficient. There should be some actual exchange for consideration before a "preexisting business relationship is established." [100]

Rotenberg believes that an opt-in regime is fair, because spamming imposes costs on the recipients of e-mail, much as an unwanted fax does. Congress had previously established an opt-in system for fax solicitations, because recipients had to pay for paper and toner, and it is not fair to impose these costs on the recipients of unwanted advertising. Rotenberg also argued that, like the law preventing "junk faxes," a federal anti-spam law should allow recipients of spam to sue spammers in small-claims court. Many consumer advocates believe that leaving the problem of spam to federal agencies is an ineffective solution: Understaffed federal agencies will have the resources to go after only the most active spammers, but smaller-scale spammers can be equally annoying.

Several state laws, which were wiped out by the passage of the CAN-SPAM Act, required that spam be labeled as such in the subject line of the e-mail. For example, the laws required all advertisements to carry the letters "ADV" in the subject line and all advertisements including adult materials to include "ADV:ADT" in the subject line. Such labels make it much easier for Internet users to identify advertisements, particularly those that could include offensive material. More importantly, such labeling requirements make it much easier for Internet users (and their parents) to set filters to block unwanted messages because the user need only set the filter to block all messages including the tags.

Although the CAN-SPAM Act ultimately included a requirement that the Federal Trade Commission, a federal agency that regulates business practices, develop requirements for labeling adult materials, many believe that a labeling requirement for all advertisements is also needed. Chris Murray of Consumers Union remarked at a House hearing that a labeling requirement would help ISPs do a better job of filtering. Without such a requirement, ISPs must guess as to what constitutes spam, thereby creating the very real danger of deleting personal e-mail. Murray gave examples of personal e-mails that had been blocked by his ISP's filtering program, suggesting that an "ADV" labeling requirement "may go a long [way] to making those filters more effective."[101]

Microsoft proposed a slight variation on ADV labeling requirements, suggesting instead that the government support the development of standards for e-mail senders, much like a "Good Housekeeping Seal of Approval," that would ensure e-mails bearing the organization's approval met certain standards, such as advertising truthfully and complying with requests to be removed from mailing lists. Under Microsoft's proposal, senders of commercial e-mail would either have to belong to an organization with clear standards or would have to label their e-mails with the "ADV" tag. As Microsoft attorney Ira Rubinstein explained: "[We] are not proposing a stand-alone ADV requirement; rather, we see it as a means to drive the widespread adoption of e-mail best practices."[102]

Anti-spam laws are constitutional.

Critics of the CAN-SPAM Act and other anti-spam laws, including marketers and civil libertarians, believe that such laws violate the First Amendment, which prohibits Congress from passing any law suppressing free speech. Many people who hate spam also worry that anti-spam laws will not survive First Amendment challenges. The Supreme Court, however, has allowed limited restrictions on commercial speech, such as advertising, and the laws' supporters believe that they fall within the established boundaries of the Court's First Amendment rulings.

Defending the CAN-SPAM Act, Congressman Billy Tauzin of Louisiana distinguished between restricting a person from saying something on the one hand and protecting people from having to listen to them saying it, on the other. He said:

> I have been asked is this an attack on the First Amendment, the free speech amendment? It is not. This is about the right to listen or not listen. Husbands understand that. We call that selective hearing, and wives get real angry with us when we do it. But Americans have always enjoyed the right to turn it off, not to hear, not to listen. That doesn't affect people's right to speak. They can speak all they want. You don't have to listen if you don't want.[103]

Although Tauzin's comments were somewhat tongue-in-cheek, the right "not to listen" does have some basis in constitutional law. Many people have compared the CAN-SPAM Act, particularly the "do-not-spam" registry, to a similar federal law allowing the creation of a "do-not-call" list allowing people to shield themselves from sales calls. Since most people would consider telemarketing calls much more invasive than spam, the same principles apply. Therefore, some legal experts believe that a federal court's ruling upholding the do-not-call list is a good indicator that anti-spam laws are constitutional. In *Mainstream Marketing* v. *Federal Trade Commission*, the appeals court ruled:

> The national do-not-call registry offers consumers a tool with which they can protect their homes against intrusions that Congress has determined to be particularly invasive. Just as a consumer can avoid door-to-door peddlers by placing a "No Solicitation" sign in his or her front yard, the

FROM THE BENCH

Court Upholds National Do-not-Call Registry

[The] national do-not-call registry is designed to reduce intrusions into personal privacy and the risk of telemarketing fraud and abuse that accompany unwanted telephone solicitation. The registry directly advances those goals. So far, more than 50 million telephone numbers have been registered on the do-not-call list, and the do-not-call regulations protect these households from receiving most unwanted telemarketing calls. According to the telemarketers' own estimate, 2.64 telemarketing calls per week—or more than 137 calls annually—were directed at an average consumer before the do-not-call list came into effect. Accordingly, absent the do-not-call registry, telemarketers would call those consumers who have already signed up for the registry an estimated total of 6.85 billion times each year.

To be sure, the do-not-call list will not block all of these calls. Nevertheless, it will prohibit a substantial number of them, making it difficult to fathom how the registry could be called an "ineffective" means of stopping invasive or abusive calls, or a regulation that "furnish[es] only speculative or marginal support" for the government's interests. Furthermore, the do-not-call list prohibits not only a significant number of commercial sales calls, but also a significant percentage of all calls causing the problems that Congress sought to address (whether commercial, charitable or political). The record demonstrates that a substantial share of all solicitation calls will be governed by the do-not-call rules. The high volume and unexpected nature of commercial calls subject to the national do-not-call registry makes those calls more problematic than nonprofit calls and solicitations based on established business relationships.

[The Federal Trade Commission (FTC)] has found that commercial callers are more likely than noncommercial callers to engage in deceptive and abusive practices ("When a pure commercial transaction is at stake, callers have an incentive to engage in all the things that telemarketers are hated for. But noncommercial speech is a different matter."). Specifically, the FTC concluded that in charitable and political calls, a significant purpose of the call is to sell a cause, not merely to receive a donation, and that noncommercial callers thus have stronger incentives not to alienate the people they call or to engage in abusive and deceptive practices.

Source: *Mainstream Marketing Services, Inc.* v. *Federal Trade Commission*, No. 03-1429 (10th Cir., Feb. 17, 2004).

do-not-call registry lets consumers avoid unwanted sales pitches that invade the home via telephone, if they choose to do so. We are convinced that the First Amendment does not prevent the government from giving consumers this option.[104]

Previously, the Supreme Court had ruled that any restrictions of commercial speech must meet three requirements to comply with the First Amendment: (1) the restrictions on speech must be based on a "substantial interest," rather than lawmakers' bias or personal beliefs; (2) the restrictions must be effective; and (3) the restrictions must be "narrowly tailored" instead of unnecessarily limiting too much speech.[105] In the *Mainstream Marketing* case, the appeals court ruled, "[The] do-not-call list directly advances the government's interests—reducing intrusions upon consumer privacy and the risk of fraud or abuse—by restricting a substantial number (and also a substantial percentage) of the calls that cause these problems."[106] The court also ruled that the list was narrowly tailored because "it does not over-regulate protected speech; rather, it restricts only calls that are targeted at unwilling recipients."[107] Like the do-not-call list, supporters of anti-spam laws say that these laws represent constitutional attempts to protect everyone's right "not to listen."

- **Should there be a right "not to listen"? Does that defeat the purpose of free speech or further it?**

Summary

Although the CAN-SPAM Act addresses pornographic and fraudulent spam, which are the most offensive types of spam, some say that stronger laws are needed. Defending their constitutionality, supporters of anti-spam laws say that they protect the usefulness of e-mail and uphold the right "not to listen."

Can the Internet Be Tamed?

L ike the Wild West of the nineteenth century, the Internet can be a very difficult area to patrol, but some law enforcement officials want to ride to the rescue like sheriffs wearing white hats. Unlike the inhabitants of the Old West, however, many "netizens" are not in favor of law enforcement officials encroaching upon their turf. Many Internet users would prefer, in fact, for the government to let the Internet police itself. People have already developed computer software that can be used to combat pornography, file swapping, and spam.

Today, the American frontier is technological rather than geographical. Noting that the Internet "empower[s] us all to share knowledge, ideas, thoughts, humor, music, words, and art with friends, strangers, and future generations," the San Francisco-based Electronic Frontier Foundation is one group that believes that the government should keep its nose out of the Internet.

On its website, the group complains that "governments and corporate interests worldwide are trying to prevent us from communicating freely through new technologies, just as when those in positions of power controlled the production and distribution of—or even burned—books they did not want people to read in the Middle Ages."[108] Many civil libertarians believe that the Internet truly is "cyberspace"—a vast area that cannot and should not be regulated because it is outside of the control of any government.

• Do you think that politicians will ever understand the Internet?

Other groups take a more earthly view of the Internet. They believe that the computers, wires, and software that make up the Internet have a physical presence in the United States and therefore can be regulated like any product. More importantly, people who post and access information on the Internet are citizens subject to laws like any other citizen are. In a brief to the Supreme Court, the conservative American Center for Law and Justice (ACLJ) acknowledged that policing the Internet is difficult, writing:

> The Internet has become an extremely controversial and difficult area to legislate since the technology is ever-changing. Publishing over the Internet, unlike in other forms of media such as print, broadcast, and video, is relatively inexpensive. Moreover, no one agency or government body watches over the content of what is placed on the Internet. The result is an open unregulated medium of communication that is highly effective.[109]

In contrast to groups like the Electronic Frontier Foundation, the ACLJ does not believe that an unregulated Internet is beneficial for society. It argued: "Unfortunately, the factors that make [the Internet] effective also make it dangerous. The Internet is becoming the fastest growing medium for pornography distribution, and some have characterized it as the best hunting ground for pedophiles."[110] Urging the Court to uphold the Child Online Protection Act (COPA), which would impose penalties on operators of pornographic websites for allowing access to minors, the ACLJ argued that "policy making is the prerogative of Congress,"[111] which has the authority to regulate the operation of the Internet within the nation's borders.

Is zoning a possibility?

Many people believe that the true issue is not whether the Internet *should* be regulated but whether it *can* be regulated. For each type of offense that can be committed on the Internet, some violators can escape the reach of the law. Some have the technological savvy to avoid punishment by concealing their identities electronically. Others are simply not within the jursidiction of U.S. law enforcement officials. For example, KaZaA moved its operations to the island nation of Vanuatu as the United States and other nations began to crack down on the manufacturers of song-swapping software. Similarly, spammers, child pornographers, online casinos, and others whom the government would like to regulate can all locate their operations in nations unwilling to cooperate with U.S. authorities.

Some people have suggested that although it is impossible to control the content of the Internet, it might be possible to "zone" cyberspace. In the same way that cities have designated "red light districts" for strip clubs and adult bookstores, some have supported relegating offensive material to a particular segment of the Internet. For example, all adult websites would be given "xxx" addresses instead of "www" addresses. Such a system would make the operation of filtering software much easier. When the Supreme Court first considered the question of Internet content regulation in 1997, Justice O'Connor embraced the general concept of Internet zoning, writing:

I view the Communications Decency Act of 1996 (CDA) as little more than an attempt by Congress to create "adult zones" on the Internet. Our precedent indicates that the creation of such zones can be constitutionally sound. Despite the soundness of its purpose, however, portions of the CDA are unconstitutional because they stray from the blueprint our prior cases have developed for constructing a "zoning law" that passes constitutional muster.[112]

Justice O'Connor acknowledged, however, that at the time, technology did not exist that would enable this type of zoning to take place.

- **Would having a "red light district" on the Internet only attract curious onlookers?**

Years have passed since the case involving the CDA, and many people believe that programmers could easily develop the technology necessary for "Internet zoning." One person who strongly supports Internet zoning is law professor Lawrence Lessig, whose views influenced Justice O'Connor's written opinion. In a law review article co-written with a computer science professor, Lessig suggests that an effective and less burdensome way to zone the Internet would be to develop a method of using "Kids-Mode Browsers."[113] Parents who wanted to protect their children from objectionable Internet content could limit their children's Internet use to these Kids-Mode Browsers, which would not load any websites labeled as adults-only. It would be up to the publishers of websites to label their sites as adults-only, but doing so would make them immune from legal liability. Therefore, website publishers would have the incentive to comply with the zoning plan.

Lessig and his co-author write that the use of Kids-Mode Browsers would have many advantages. Website publishers could easily comply with the adults-only labeling requirement, and their sites would be blocked only to people who specifically decided to install Kids-Mode Browsers. A labeling system would be much cheaper and easier than verifying the age of every person surfing the web, a requirement imposed by many of Congress's attempts at regulating Internet content.

Of course, establishing zoning requirements poses threats. ISPs could be pressured by prosecutors or conservative religious groups into blocking access to adults-only sites, not only for people with Kids-Mode Browsers but for all subscribers.

FROM THE BENCH

Justice O'Connor Suggests Zoning the Internet

[An] adult zone, once created, would succeed in preserving adults' access while denying minors' access to the regulated speech. Before today, there was no reason to question this assumption, for the Court has previously only considered laws that operated in the physical world, a world that with two characteristics that make it possible to create "adult zones": geography and identity. A minor can see an adult dance show only if he enters an establishment that provides such entertainment. And should he attempt to do so, the minor will not be able to conceal completely his identity (or, consequently, his age). Thus, the twin characteristics of geography and identity enable the establishment's proprietor to prevent children from entering the establishment, but to let adults inside.

The electronic world is fundamentally different. Because it is no more than the interconnection of electronic pathways, cyberspace allows speakers and listeners to mask their identities. Cyberspace undeniably reflects some form of geography; chat rooms and Websites, for example, exist at fixed "locations" on the Internet. Since users can transmit and receive messages on the Internet without revealing anything about their identities or ages, however, it is not currently possible to exclude persons from accessing certain messages on the basis of their identity.

Cyberspace differs from the physical world in another basic way: Cyberspace is malleable. Thus, it is possible to construct barriers in cyberspace and use them to screen for identity, making cyberspace more like the physical world and, consequently, more amenable to zoning laws. This transformation of cyberspace is already underway. Internet speakers (users who post material on the Internet)

Such a system would raise many of the same objections as have been raised to laws such as the CDA—that adults should be allowed to view adult materials and that sexual health-related information would be blocked. Not everyone is convinced that zoning will protect free speech. Laurence O'Toole, criticizing British efforts to block pornographic material by pressuring ISPs, writes that the "Internet might be censor-proof," meaning that there is no way to prevent information from being placed on the Internet. He believes, however, zoning will lead to that

have begun to zone cyberspace itself through the use of "gateway" technology. Such technology requires Internet users to enter information about themselves—perhaps an adult identification number or a credit card number—before they can access certain areas of cyberspace, much like a bouncer checks a person's driver's license before admitting him to a nightclub. Internet users who access information have not attempted to zone cyberspace itself, but have tried to limit their own power to access information in cyberspace, much as a parent controls what her children watch on television by installing a lock box. This user based zoning is accomplished through the use of screening software (such as Cyber Patrol or SurfWatch).

Although the prospects for the eventual zoning of the Internet appear promising, I agree with the Court that we must evaluate the constitutionality of the CDA as it applies to the Internet as it exists today.... Given the present state of cyberspace, I agree with the Court that the "display" provision cannot pass muster. Until gateway technology is available throughout cyberspace, and it is not in 1997, a speaker cannot be reasonably assured that the speech he displays will reach only adults because it is impossible to confine speech to an "adult zone." Thus, the only way for a speaker to avoid liability under the CDA is to refrain completely from using indecent speech. But this forced silence impinges on the First Amendment right of adults to make and obtain this speech and, for all intents and purposes, "reduce[s] the adult population [on the Internet] to reading only what is fit for children."

Source: *Reno* v. *ACLU*, 521 U.S. 884 (1997; O'Connor, J., concurring in the judgment in part and dissenting in part)

information being blocked from large segments of the population. He writes:

> Smart techno-types may well route around the roadblocks, but as the internet achieves a far larger presence as a mass media, populated by the technically challenged, a degree of censorship for the many will have prevailed.[114]

Will technology prevail?

Ultimately, policing the Internet using traditional law enforcement methods might prove to be too difficult to be worth pursuing. Passing a law in Congress takes months or years of debate, and technology simply moves too fast for lawmakers and prosecutors to keep up. People find new ways to bend the laws or avoid detection. Additionally, as peer-to-peer networking develops, the content of the Internet is increasingly being created by huge numbers of people—far too many people for courts to try or prisons to hold. Many believe that while law enforcement officials cannot keep up, computer programmers in proverbial "white hats" might be able to. Perhaps government resources would be better spent offering incentives to software developers to produce new products that police the Internet more effectively than law enforcement officials can.

- **Should the government leave regulation of the Internet to computer programmers?**

Explaining why technological approaches are the only sensible means of combating copyright infringement on peer-to-peer networks, MediaDefender CEO Randy Saaf told Congress:

> The most threatening aspect of P2P networking to the copyright holders is the growing trend of decentralization. All of the most popular P2P networking technologies in the world are either completely or partially decentralized. Decentralization

means that there is no central entity to sue or regulate using the law. Even if all the courts agreed to shut a decentralized network down, it could not be done because it is simply a free floating technology protocol on the Internet. . . . Often times MediaDefender's technological solutions [represent] the only way to prevent immediate irreparable economic harm when a highly anticipated piece of copyrighted material is leaked onto the Internet. Nobody really wants to sue individuals or programmers. The financial loss has already occurred by the time the lawsuit is over, and the infringer is rarely able to correct the loss to the copyright holder. With tens of millions of P2P users, most of which are in the United States, many people we know and love are downloading pirated material.[115]

Summary

Despite new interest in traveling to Mars, the Internet is truly the new American frontier. Although Congress has tried to police the content of the Internet, it is a rapidly growing and complicated network that has taken on a life of its own. Rather than trying to regulate the content of the Internet, some have suggested that more sensible approaches would be to create adults-only zones and to support technological measures for patrolling Internet content.

1. *U.S.* v. *Alkhabaz (aka Jake Baker)*, 890 F. Supp. 1375 (E.D. Mich. 1995).

2. Brief for Amicus Curiae Jane Doe, *U.S.* v. *Alkhabaz (aka Jake Baker)*, 104 F.3d 1492 (6th Cir. 1997).

3. Ibid.

4. Brief for Amicus Curiae American Civil Liberties Union, *U.S.* v. *Alkhabaz (aka Jake Baker)*, 104 F.3d 1492 (6th Cir. 1997).

5. Ibid.

6. Ibid.

7. *Reno* v. *ACLU*, 521 U.S. 884 (1997).

8. Ibid.

9. *U.S.* v. *American Library Association*, No. 02-361 (June 23, 2003).

10. Nadine Strossen, *Defending Pornography*. New York: Scribner, 1995, p. 248.

11. Ibid.

12. Adam Thierer, "New Wind in the Sails of the Censorship Crusade?" *TechKnowledge* (July 6, 2001). A publication of the Cato Institute.

13. Ibid.

14. Ibid.

15. Lawrence Walters, "Top Five Reasons Why Obscenity Laws Are Inappropriate in the Digital Age," *http://www.firstamendment.com/ pubs_topfive-03-30-01.php3*.

16. Philip D. Harvey, *The Government* v. *Erotica*. Amherst, N.Y.: Prometheus Books, 2001, p. 226.

17. *Miller* v. *California*, 418 U.S. 915 (1974).

18. *Ashcroft* v. *ACLU*, No. 00-1293 (May 13, 2002; Stevens, J., dissenting).

19. Lawrence Walters, "Top Five Reasons."

20. *U.S.* v. *American Library Association*, No. 02-361 (June 23, 2003; opinion of Rehnquist, J.).

21. Edward R. Johnson, "Statement on Compulsory Internet Filtering" (Sept. 4, 2003), *http://www.library .okstate.edu/Dean/netfilter.htm*.

22. J. Douglas Archer, "Internet Filtering," *Advance* (Spring 2002). A publication of the University of Notre Dame library system.

23. Brief for American Library Association, *U.S.* v. *American Library Association*, No. 02-361 (June 23, 2003).

24. Ibid.

25. Ibid.

26. Archer, "Internet Filtering."

27. Donald E. Wildmon, *The Case Against Pornography*. Wheaton, Ill.: Victor Books, 1986, p. 89.

28. Ibid., p. 91.

29. See *http://www.victimsofpornography.org/*.

30. Andrea Dworkin, "Against the Male Flood," in *Pornography, Sex Work, and Hate Speech*. New York, Garland Publishing, 1997.

31. Catherine A. MacKinnon, "Not a Moral Issue," in *Pornography, Sex Work, and Hate Speech*.

32. Cong. Rec. H9735 (Oct. 20, 2003; statement of Rep. Osborne).

33. Ibid.

34. Brief for Amicus Curiae American Center for Law and Justice, *Ashcroft* v. *ACLU*, No. 00-1293 (May 13, 2002).

35. *Ashcroft* v. *ACLU*, No. 00-1293 (May 13, 2002; opinion of Thomas, J.).

36. Brief for Amicus Curiae Public Libraries, *U.S.* v. *American Library Association*, No. 02-361 (June 23, 2003).

37. Kathryn Kolbert and Zak Mettger, *Justice Talking—Censoring the Web*. New York: New Press, 2001.

38. Computer Policy (proposed), Southern Utah University. See *http://www.suu.edu/ faculty/lewis_t/computerpolicy.htm*.

39. Ibid.

40. Brief for Amicus Curiae American Center for Law and Justice, *U.S.* v. *American Library Association*, No. 02-361 (June 23, 2003).

41. Declaration of DJ Xealot, *A&M Records, Inc.* v. *Napster, Inc.*, 114 F. Supp.2d 896 (N.D. Cal. 2000).

42. U.S. Const. art. I § 8.

43. *Metro-Goldwyn Mayer Studios, Inc. v. Grokster,* 259 F. Supp.2d 1029 (C.D. Cal. 2003).

44. *Piracy of Intellectual Property on Peer-to-Peer Networks: Hearing Before the House Subcommittee on Court, the Internet, and Intellectual Property,* 107th Cong. (2002).

45. *Sony Corp. v. Universal City Studios, Inc.,* 464 U.S. 417 (1984).

46. Ibid.

47. Robert Leitman, "Americans Think Downloading Music for Personal Use Is an Innocent Act," *The Harris Poll* 5 (Jan. 28, 2004).

48. Plaintiff's Answer to Complaint in *Sony Music Entertainment Inc. v. Raymond Maalouf,* No. C 03 4085 EMC ADR (N.D. Cal. 2003).

49. Ibid.

50. Expert Report of Robert E. Hall, *A & M Records, Inc. v. Napster, Inc.,* 114 F. Supp.2d 896 (N.D. Cal. 2000).

51. Declaration of Chuck D, *A & M Records, Inc. v. Napster, Inc.,* 114 F. Supp.2d 896 (N.D. Cal.2000).

52. Ibid.

53. Ibid.

54. Brief Amicus Curiae for Eagle Forum and Association of American Physicians and Surgeons, *A & M Records, Inc. v. Napster, Inc.,* 114 F. Supp.2d 896 (N.D. Cal.2000).

55. Ibid.

56. House Subcommittee, *Piracy of Intellectual Property.*

57. Ibid.

58. Ibid.

59. Michael Singer, "Calif. Lawmaker Calls for Internet Vigilantism," *Internetnews.com* (June 26, 2002).

60. Ibid.

61. House Subcommittee, *Piracy of Intellectual Property.*

62. *Leiber v. Grokster,* No. 03-55901 (9th Cir. 2004).

63. *A&M Records, Inc. v. Napster, Inc.,* 114 F. Supp.2d 896 (N.D. Cal.2000).

64. *Music on the Internet: Hearing Before the House Subcommittee on the Courts, the Internet, and Intellectual Property,* 107th Cong. (2001).

65. Ibid.

66. House Subcommittee, *Piracy of Intellectual Property.*

67. Ibid.

68. Ibid.

69. Ibid.

70. Ibid.

71. *Metro-Goldwyn Mayer Studios, Inc. v. Grokster,* 259 F. Supp.2d 1029 (C.D. Cal. 2003).

72. *Recording Industry Assn. of America v. Verizon Internet Services,* No. 03-7015 (D.C. Cir. Dec. 19, 2003).

73. House Subcommittee, *Piracy of Intellectual Property.*

74. Ibid.

75. Ibid.

76. *The Complete Monty Python's Flying Circus: All the Words,* vol. 2. New York: Pantheon Books, 1989, p. 27.

77. *Spam (Unsolicited Commercial E-Mail): Hearing Before the Senate Committee on Commerce, Science, and Transportation,* 108th Cong. (2003).

78. Ibid.

79. Ibid.

80. Ibid.

81. Anita Ramasastry, "Why the New Federal CAN Spam Law Probably Won't Work," *Findlaw's Writ* (Dec. 3, 2003).

82. Senate Committee, *Spam.*

83. *Reduction in Distribution of Spam Act: Hearing Before the House Subcommittee on Crime, Terrorism, and Homeland Security.* 108th Cong. (2003).

84. *Legislative Efforts to Combat Spam: Joint Hearing Before the House Subcommittee on Commerce, Trade, and Consumer Protection and the House Committee on Energy and Commerce,* 108th Cong. (2003).

85. Ramasastry (2003).

86. *Unsolicitied Commercial Electronic Mail Act of 2001 and the Anti-Spamming Act of 2001: Hearing Before the House Committee on the Judiciary*, 107th Cong. (2001).

87. Ramasastry (2003).

88. Comments of Center for Democracy and Technology, Federal Trade Commission Rulemaking No. P044405, *Proposed Mark for Sexually Oriented Spam* (2004).

89. Ibid.

90. House Committee, *Unsolicited Commercial Electronic Mail Act of 2001.*

91. Joint Hearing, *Legislative Efforts to Combat Spam.*

92. Ibid.

93. Ibid.

94. Ibid.

95. Ibid.

96. House Subcommittee, *Reduction in Distribution of Spam Act.*

97. Senate Committee, *Spam.*

98. House Subcommittee, *Reduction in Distribution of Spam Act.*

99. CAUCE Statement on CAN-SPAM Act (Dec. 16, 2003). See *http://www.cauce.org/ news/index.shtml.*

100. Senate Committee, *Spam.*

101. House Subcommittee, *Reduction in Distribution of Spam Act.*

102. Joint Hearing, *Legislative Efforts to Combat Spam.*

103. Ibid.

104. *Mainstream Marketing Services, Inc. v. Federal Trade Commission,* No. 03-1429 (10th Cir., Feb. 17, 2004)

105. *Central Hudson Gas & Electric Co. v. Public Service Commission,* 447 U.S. 557 (1980).

106. *Mainstream Marketing,* No. 03-11429.

107. Ibid.

108. See *http://www.eff.org/about/.*

109. Brief for Amicus Curiae American Center for Law and Justice, *Ashcroft* v. *ACLU,* No. 03-218 (2003).

110. Ibid.

111. Ibid.

112. *Reno* v. *ACLU,* 521 U.S. 884 (1997).

113. Lawrence Lessig and Paul Resnick, "Zoning Speech on the Internet: A Legal and Technical Model," *Michigan Law Review* 98 (1999).

114. Laurence O'Toole, *Pornocopia: Porn, Sex, Technology, and Desire.* New York: Serpent's Tail, 1998, p. 272.

115. House Subcommittee, *Piracy of Intellectual Property.*

Books

Harvey, Philip D. *The Government vs. Erotica.* Amherst, N.Y.: Prometheus Books, 2001.

Kolbert, Kathryn, and Zak Mettger. *Justice Talking—Censoring the Web.* New York: New Press, 2001.

Maschke, Karen, ed. *Pornography, Sex Work, and Hate Speech.* New York: Garland Publishing, 1997.

O'Toole, Laurence. *Pornocopia: Porn, Sex, Technology, and Desire.* New York: Serpent's Tail, 1998.

Strossen, Nadine. *Defending Pornography.* New York: Scribner, 1995.

Wildmon, Donald E. *The Case Against Pornography,* Wheaton, Ill.: Victor Books, 1986.

Websites

American Center for Law and Justice
http://www.aclj.org/
This public interest law firm is devoted to religious conservative causes, including combating pornography.

American Civil Liberties Union
http://www.aclu.org
This national organization promotes free speech and other civil liberties through litigation, lobbying, and public education.

American Library Association
http://www.ala.org
This national association of libraries opposes mandatory Internet filtering.

Cato Institute
http://www.cato.org
This Libertarian think-tank is opposed to government regulation generally, including restrictions on Internet use and content.

Center for Democracy and Technology
http://www.cdt.org
This is a liberal group that favors broad protection for online speech.

Center for the Community Interest
http://www.communityinterest.org
This is a conservative group dedicated to strengthening measures to combat quality-of-life crimes such as drug use and pornography.

Consumers Union
http://www.consumersunion.org
This is a nonprofit consumer advocacy organization that publishes *Consumer Reports.*

Electronic Frontier Foundation
http://www.eff.org
This liberal group uses litigation and advocacy to reduce restrictions on Internet communication, including file sharing.

Electronic Privacy Information Center
http://www.epic.org
This advocacy group favors measures to protect personal privacy in the information age. It favors strong restrictions on spam.

Federal Trade Commission
http://www.ftc.gov
This federal agency is in charge of enforcing consumer protections, including federal anti-spam laws.

Morality in Media
http://www.moralityinmedia.org
This is an anti-pornography group that favors restrictions on content of broadcast media and the Internet.

National Law Center for Children and Families
http://www.nationallawcenter.org
This is a conservative public interest law firm that is active in antipornography litigation.

Public Knowledge
http://www.publicknowledge.org
This is an advocacy group seeking to expand the "public domain" of uncopyrighted materials and expand "fair use" rights, including file sharing on peer-to-peer networks.

Recording Industry Association of America
http://www.riaa.org
This is a trade association representing record labels. It is active in court battles against unauthorized file sharing on peer-to-peer networks.

Case Law and Legislation

A&M Records, Inc. v. Napster, Inc., 114 F. Supp.2d 896 (N.D. Cal. 2000)
Held that Napster was liable for copyright infringement on its peer-to-peer
network because it posted a list of copyrighted material that was available for
unauthorized copying.

Ashcroft v. ACLU, No. 00-1293 (May 13, 2002)
This case barred the government from enforcing COPA until more information
could be gathered about its impact. However, the case acknowledged that the law
could be constitutional.

Child Online Protection Act (COPA)
This act bans commercial Websites from making material that is "harmful to
minors" available to minors.

Children's Internet Protection Act (CIPA)
This act requires public libraries to install filtering software that blocks
pornography in order to receive federal funding for Internet access.

Communications Decency Act (CDA)
This act banned making "indecent" material available to minors via the Internet.

Digital Millennium Copyright Act
This updated federal copyright law gives copyright owners new control over
digital copies of their works, including new tools to fight the posting of pirated
material on the Web.

Mainstream Marketing Services, Inc. v. Federal Trade Commission,
No. 03-1429 (10th Cir. 2004)
An appeal court ruled that a national do-not-call list was a constitutional regulation
of commercial speech.

Metro-Goldyn Mayer Studios, Inc. v. Grokster, 259 F. Supp.2d 1029
(C.D. Cal. 2003)
In this case, a trial judge ruled that Grokster and StreamCast were not liable
for copyright infringement by users of their peer-to-peer software because the
companies had no way of knowing which files were being traded.

Miller v. California, 418 U.S. 915 (1974)
The Supreme Court rules that the First Amendment does not protect obscenity,
which is defined as being patently offensive, appealing to prurient interests, and
having no serious value.

123

Recording Industry Assn. of America v. *Verizon Internet Services,*
No. 03-7015 (D.C. Cir. 2003)
An appeals court ruled that RIAA could not use a streamlined subpoena process
to obtain the names of song swappers from their Internet Service Providers.

Reno v. *ACLU,* 521 U.S. 884 (1997)
This case declared the Communications Decency Act unconstitutional.

U.S. v. *Alkhabaz* (*aka Jake Baker*), 890 F. Supp. 1375 (E.D. Mich. 1995)
This federal trial court dismisses criminal threat charges against a man who
posted on a newsgroup a violent sex fantasy about a classmate.

U.S. v. *American Library Association,* No. 02-361 (June 23, 2003)
This case upheld CIPA's restrictions on library funding.

Terms and Concepts

Academic freedom

Copyright

E-mail filters

Fair use

File sharing

Filtering software

Harmful to minors

Indecent

Infringement

Interdiction

Internet

Internet Service Provider (ISP)

Internet zoning

Marketplace of ideas

Obscene

Opt-in

Opt-out

Overblocking

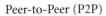

Peer-to-Peer (P2P)

Pornography

Royalty

Self-help

Server

Spam

Spoofing

Transaction costs

Victimless crime

World Wide Web

Beginning Legal Research

The goal of POINT/COUNTERPOINT is not only to provide the reader with an introduction to a controversial issue affecting society, but also to encourage the reader to explore the issue more fully. This appendix, then, is meant to serve as a guide to the reader in researching the current state of the law as well as exploring some of the public-policy arguments as to why existing laws should be changed or new laws are needed.

Like many types of research, legal research has become much faster and more accessible with the invention of the Internet. This appendix discusses some of the best starting points, but of course "surfing the Net" will uncover endless additional sources of information — some more reliable than others. Some important sources of law are not yet available on the Internet, but these can generally be found at the larger public and university libraries. Librarians usually are happy to point patrons in the right direction.

The most important source of law in the United States is the Constitution. Originally enacted in 1787, the Constitution outlines the structure of our federal government and sets limits on the types of laws that the federal government and state governments can pass. Through the centuries, a number of amendments have been added to or changed in the Constitution, most notably the first ten amendments, known collectively as the Bill of Rights, which guarantee important civil liberties. Each state also has its own constitution, many of which are similar to the U.S. Constitution. It is important to be familiar with the U.S. Constitution because so many of our laws are affected by its requirements. State constitutions often provide protections of individual rights that are even stronger than those set forth in the U.S. Constitution.

Within the guidelines of the U.S. Constitution, Congress — both the House of Representatives and the Senate — passes bills that are either vetoed or signed into law by the President. After the passage of the law, it becomes part of the United States Code, which is the official compilation of federal laws. The state legislatures use a similar process, in which bills become law when signed by the state's governor. Each state has its own official set of laws, some of which are published by the state and some of which are published by commercial publishers. The U.S. Code and the state codes are an important source of legal research; generally, legislators make efforts to make the language of the law as clear as possible.

However, reading the text of a federal or state law generally provides only part of the picture. In the American system of government, after the legislature passes laws and the executive (U.S. President or state governor) signs them, it is up to the judicial branch of the government, the court system, to interpret the laws and decide whether they violate any provision of the Constitution. At the state level, each state's supreme court has the ultimate authority in determining what a law means and whether or not it violates the state constitution. However, the federal courts—headed by the U.S. Supreme Court—can review state laws and court decisions to determine whether they violate federal laws or the U.S. Constitution. For example, a state court may find that a particular criminal law is valid under the state's constitution, but a federal court may then review the state court's decision and determine that the law is invalid under the U.S. Constitution.

It is important, then, to read court decisions when doing legal research. The Constitution uses language that is intentionally very general—for example, prohibiting "unreasonable searches and seizures" by the police—and court cases often provide more guidance. For example, the U.S. Supreme Court's 2001 decision in *Kyllo* v. *United States* held that scanning the outside of a person's house using a heat sensor to determine whether the person is growing marijuana is unreasonable—*if* it is done without a search warrant secured from a judge. Supreme Court decisions provide the most definitive explanation of the law of the land, and it is therefore important to include these in research. Often, when the Supreme Court has not decided a case on a particular issue, a decision by a federal appeals court or a state supreme court can provide guidance; but just as laws and constitutions can vary from state to state, so can federal courts be split on a particular interpretation of federal law or the U.S. Constitution. For example, federal appeals courts in Louisiana and California may reach opposite conclusions in similar cases.

Lawyers and courts refer to statutes and court decisions through a formal system of citations. Use of these citations reveals which court made the decision (or which legislature passed the statute) and when and enables the reader to locate the statute or court case quickly in a law library. For example, the legendary Supreme Court case *Brown* v. *Board of Education* has the legal citation 347 U.S. 483 (1954). At a law library, this 1954 decision can be found on page 483 of volume 347 of the U.S. Reports, the official collection of the Supreme Court's decisions. Citations can also be helpful in locating court cases on the Internet.

Understanding the current state of the law leads only to a partial understanding of the issues covered by the POINT/COUNTERPOINT series. For a fuller understanding of the issues, it is necessary to look at public-policy arguments that the current state of the law is not adequately addressing the issue. Many groups lobby for new legislation or changes to existing legislation; the National Rifle Association (NRA), for example, lobbies Congress and the state legislatures constantly to make existing gun control laws less restrictive and not to pass additional laws. The NRA and other groups dedicated to various causes might also intervene in pending court cases: a group such as Planned Parenthood might file a brief *amicus curiae* (as "a friend of the court")—called an "amicus brief"—in a lawsuit that could affect abortion rights. Interest groups also use the media to influence public opinion, issuing press releases and frequently appearing in interviews on news programs and talk shows. The books in POINT/COUNTERPOINT list some of the interest groups that are active in the issue at hand, but in each case there are countless other groups working at the local, state, and national levels. It is important to read everything with a critical eye, for sometimes interest groups present information in a way that can be read only to their advantage. The informed reader must always look for bias.

Finding sources of legal information on the Internet is relatively simple thanks to "portal" sites such as FindLaw (*www.findlaw.com*), which provides access to a variety of constitutions, statutes, court opinions, law review articles, news articles, and other resources—including all Supreme Court decisions issued since 1893. Other useful sources of information include the U.S. Government Printing Office (*www.gpo.gov*), which contains a complete copy of the U.S. Code, and the Library of Congress's THOMAS system (*thomas.loc.gov*), which offers access to bills pending before Congress as well as recently passed laws. Of course, the Internet changes every second of every day, so it is best to do some independent searching. Most cases, studies, and opinions that are cited or referred to in public debate can be found online—and *everything* can be found in one library or another.

The Internet can provide a basic understanding of most important legal issues, but not all sources can be found there. To find some documents it is necessary to visit the law library of a university or a public law library; some cities have public law libraries, and many library systems keep legal documents at the main branch. On the following page are some common citation forms.

COMMON CITATION FORMS

Source of Law	Sample Citation	Notes
U.S. Supreme Court	*Employment Division* v. *Smith*, 485 U.S. 660 (1988)	The U.S. Reports is the official record of Supreme Court decisions. There is also an unofficial Supreme Court ("S.Ct.") reporter.
U.S. Court of Appeals	*United States* v. *Lambert*, 695 F.2d 536 (11th Cir.1983)	Appellate cases appear in the Federal Reporter, designated by "F." The 11th Circuit has jurisdiction in Alabama, Florida, and Georgia.
U.S. District Court	*Carillon Importers, Ltd.* v. *Frank Pesce Group, Inc.*, 913 F.Supp. 1559 (S.D.Fla.1996)	Federal trial-level decisions are reported in the Federal Supplement ("F.Supp."). Some states have multiple federal districts; this case originated in the Southern District of Florida.
U.S. Code	Thomas Jefferson Commemoration Commission Act, 36 U.S.C., §149 (2002)	Sometimes the popular names of legislation — names with which the public may be familiar — are included with the U.S. Code citation.
State Supreme Court	*Sterling* v. *Cupp*, 290 Ore. 611, 614, 625 P.2d 123, 126 (1981)	The Oregon Supreme Court decision is reported in both the state's reporter and the Pacific regional reporter.
State statute	Pennsylvania Abortion Control Act of 1982, 18 Pa. Cons. Stat. 3203-3220 (1990)	States use many different citation formats for their statutes.

131

page:
76: Associated Press, AP
99: Associated Press, AP

Cover: Associated Press, AP

ALAN MARZILLI, of Durham, North Carolina, is an independent consultant working on several ongoing projects for state and federal government agencies and nonprofit organizations. He has spoken about mental health issues in more than twenty states, the District of Columbia, and Puerto Rico; his work includes training mental health administrators, nonprofit management and staff, and people with mental illness and their family members on a wide variety of topics, including effective advocacy, community-based mental health services, and housing. He has written several handbooks and training curricula that are used nationally. He managed statewide and national mental health advocacy programs and worked for several public interest lobbying organizations in Washington, D.C., while studying law at Georgetown University.